TRUTH FOR TODAY SERIES

THE WONDER OF WORSHIP

A Biblical Guide for the Worshiper

Stephen Phifer

Copyright © 2024 by Steve Phifer

All rights reserved. No part of this publication may be reproduced, distributed, or transmitted in any form or by any means, including photocopying, recording, or other electronic or mechanical methods, without the prior written permission of the publisher, except in the case of brief quotations embodied in critical reviews and certain other noncommercial uses permitted by copyright law. For permission requests, write to the publisher at publishing@kingdomwinds.com.

Unless otherwise indicated, all Scripture references are taken from the Holy Bible, New International Version® Copyright © 1973, 1978, 1984, 2011 by Biblica, Inc.® Used by permission. All rights reserved worldwide.

Scripture marked NKJV taken from the New King James Version®. Copyright © 1982 by Thomas Nelson. Used by permission. All rights reserved.

Scripture marked MEV taken from The Holy Bible, Modern English Version. Copyright © 2014 by Military Bible Association. Published and distributed by Charisma House.

Scripture marked RSV taken from the Revised Standard Version of the Bible, copyright © 1946, 1952, and 1971 the Division of Christian Education of the National Council of the Churches of Christ in the United States of America. Used by permission. All rights reserved.

Scripture marked ESV taken from The Holy Bible, English Standard Version. ESV® Text Edition: 2016. Copyright © 2001 by Crossway Bibles, a publishing ministry of Good News Publishers.

Scripture marked ASV taken from the American Standard Version in the Public Domain

Scripture marked NASB taken from the New American Standard Bible®, Copyright © 1960, 1971, 1977, 1995, 2020 by The Lockman Foundation. All rights reserved.

First Edition, 2024

ISBN: 978-1-64590-062-7

Published by Kingdom Winds Publishing.

www.kingdomwinds.com

publishing@kingdomwinds.com

Printed in the United States of America

TABLE OF CONTENTS

AUTHOR PROFILE: Dr. Stephen Phifer	4
INTRODUCTION: "Wonderful"—"full of wonders"	5
CHAPTER 1: Finding the Book Again	13
CHAPTER 2: Praise and Worship	19
CHAPTER 3: Private Worship, Public Worship, and the Presence of God	25
CHAPTER 4: Two Lenses Required	31
CHAPTER 5: Dynamics of Spirit	35
CHAPTER 6: Dynamics of Truth	41
CHAPTER 7: Biblical Worship Music	49
CHAPTER 8: The 7 Biblical Models: 1 & 2	57
CHAPTER 9: The 7 Biblical Models 3 & 4	63
CHAPTER 10: The 7 Biblical Models 5, 6, & 7	71
CHAPTER 11: Service Structure	81
CHAPTER 12: The Sword of the Spirit	85
CONCLUSION: The Congregational Challenge	89

AUTHOR PROFILE

Dr. Stephen Phifer

I have served the Church of the Lord Jesus Christ as worship leader, worship educator, musician, and writer. Today, my ministry is one of worship renewal. I began full-time ministry in 1975, serving churches in several states and denominational and university ministries. My study of worship began in 1980 and has become the focus of my ministry. I hold bachelor's and master's degrees in music education and a doctorate in worship studies. I have guest lectured at colleges and seminaries across America and overseas. My wife, Freeda, is a marvelous musician and music educator, and she has been my flawless companion in life and ministry since June 1974.

Stephen Phifer

INTRODUCTION

> *Give unto the Lord, O you mighty ones, give unto the Lord glory and strength. Give unto the Lord the glory due to his name; worship the Lord in the beauty of holiness (Psalm 29:1–2, KJV)*

This call is universal. The stars hear it and sing. The planets move to its rhythms. Angels have their own language to line out the details of His glory, this "glory due His name" (Psalm 29:2). The hearts of men, women, boys, and girls resonate in multiplied timbres. This universal song is addressed "To Him who sits on the throne of heaven." We, God's covenant-people, are really a massive choir and orchestra assembled for this wonderful purpose of giving the Lord the glory due His name. Sometimes we give private recitals in the Secret Place of prayer, and at other times in large gatherings where a multitude or simply two or three are gathered together in His name (Matthew 118:20), we summon the whole family of faith to sing and play for His glory. This is the calling on our redeemed lives, and it is the pressing business of this hour.

How should this be done? Such an enterprise cannot be left to even our best ideas alone. There is a worship that pleases God! We find its dimensions, its demands, and its delights in the Holy Book of God, the Bible. Here we find both the context and the content our worship. With the Book, we load our hearts with eternal things so we can express them in contemporary terms, injecting a healing dose of truth into this stricken moment. There is no better use of words and tunes and voices and instruments. Our God-given creativity can find no higher purpose, no grander theme, and no more powerful text than these "wonderful words of life."[1]

How do we measure our success? Not in the applause of people, nor in any personal acclaim we may earn, nor in any other human measure. Our standard is the one found in the Heavenly Zion: "The glory due His name" (Pslam 29:2). To sense the Manifest Presence of the Lord is our goal, and to please the Lord Jesus is our purpose.

We have His complete attention. Do we give Him ours? Let us seize a fragment of time and step through the "torn veil" into an eternal moment of glory, the glory of the "only Begotten of the Father, full of grace and

---
1 Bliss, P.P. "Wonderful Words of Life." 1874.

truth" (John 1:14, NKJV). There are no clocks here. Time is suspended in the revelation of God as we feast on the manna of heaven and are strengthened by His nearness.

This is "The Wonder of Worship," and this is the subject of our study.

"Wonderful"—"full of wonders"

Congregational worship should be nothing less than wonderful—full of wonders. It should never be ordinary, feeble, boring, deceitful, theatrical, plain, dull, or uninspiring. What wonders are found in congregational worship?

- » Divine Beauty from the Holy Spirit and its earthly reflection found in the worship arts,
- » Supernatural passion that strikes fire in the human heart,
- » Truth from heaven to fill the voids in the inquiring human mind,
- » Fellowship with our Maker and with brothers and sisters likewise made by Him,
- » The Peace of Christ, which passes all understanding, comforting the believer's spirit,
- » Faith in God that transmits itself into the expectations of the worshiper,
- » Hope in the future that promises rest and worship in proper balance, and
- » Love for God and for others, thus fulfilling the two greatest commands.

Are we brave enough to inventory our worship experience in our local church? How many wonders do we find there?

If the stock is low and the variety is lacking, perhaps the worship we experience needs a new guide. On second thought, perhaps we must rescue our worship experience from contemporary culture and find more lasting, proven, and powerful truths to guide us. May I suggest the Bible? Sometimes, we approach congregational worship as if the Bible had nothing to say on the matter.

Many years ago, while serving First Assembly of God in Winston-Salem, NC, I taught a 13-week Sunday School course called "Worship that

Pleases God" twice a year. After several years of this, I had taught at least 1000 of our people a biblical vision for worship. The result? It was not difficult to lead that congregation in worship. They understood what I was doing, and, more importantly, they knew what they were doing when it was time to worship God. I assessed it this way: They approached the worship service using biblical models.

- » They were an informed Holy-Royal Priesthood (1 Peter 2:9).
- » They knew how to minister to the Lord with the Living-Sacrifice of Praise (Romans 12:1–2, Hebrews 13:15).
- » They expected their worship to bring them into His Manifest Presence before the Throne of God and of the Lamb (Psalm 22:3).
- » They knew our sanctuary had become the Lord's Office-place because (Acts 13:1)
- » The River of Life was flowing from the throne as a healing stream (Ezekiel 47, Revelation 22).

Why all these blessings?

- » Because we had celebrated our unity before God with the arts of David's Tabernacle and
- » Because we had come into the Holy of Holies by processing through Moses' Tabernacle, a faithful copy of the Heavenly Zion.

I had developed this biblical vision of worship that pleases God from a 10-year intensive study of the Scriptures. In the early 1990s, I felt directed to write this class into a book. It took another 10 years to see it come to print as *Worship that Pleases God: The Passion and Reason of True Worship* (Trafford Publishing, 2004, 2014).

The Wonder of Worship: A Biblical Guide for the Congregation is a contemporary presentation of the core truths of this biblical vision designed for class use within the congregation or for personal study by the individual worshiper. My task was and is to help the worshiper see the difference between the truth of worship and the cultural expression of worship. Worship is expressed through local, generational, and personal cultural means and is, therefore, subject to wide variations of expression. Too often, these cultural expressions (songs, musical ensembles, presentation styles, service structures, and technologies) are misjudged as the substance of worship, rather than the expressions of worship. To borrow from the words of Jesus to the Samaritan Woman-at-the-well, the human expressions of worship can be called the human spirit of worship. This "spirit" is not the Holy Spirit but is the expression of the human spirit—the God-consciousness part each of us possesses. At the same time, the Holy Spirit is at work ministering the Truth of worship found in the unchanging Word of God. This "worship in spirit and truth" is the dynamic we need (John 4:24). If we do not perceive the differences between the cultural expression of worship and the spiritual truth of worship, we may treat temporary things as if they were eternal and eternal things as if they were temporary and therefore disposable.

For these 12 sessions, we will seek the eternal, unchanging things revealed in the Word of God. Wise pastors and worship leaders can make local application through the carefully observed principles presented in this class. As a member of the Lord's Holy Church, you can take your place among the People of God to worship the Lord in Spirit and in Truth.

The Prayer of Jesus at the Last Supper

In the coming chapters, I will present seven biblical models of worship from the Scriptures. These biblical concepts help us understand public worship. At the heart of these chapters presenting these ideas: 7 Biblical Models of worship; carefully defined biblical words, phrases, and images; and powerful concepts of worship in "spirit and in truth," lies a powerful prayer from the heart of Jesus for His church. On His last night with the disciples, after their Last Supper was completed, Jesus prayed for us. John records it in chapter 17 of his Gospel.

> *My prayer is not for them alone. I pray also for those who will believe in me through their message, that all of them may be one, Father, just as you are in me and I am in you. May they also be in us so that the world may believe that you have sent me. I have given them the glory that you gave me, that they may be one as we are one: I in them and you in me—so that they may be brought to complete unity. Then the world will know that you sent me and have loved them even as you have loved me. (John 17:20–23)*

Can we recognize the standard of this unity? It is the most thorough and complete unity possible, that of the Divine Godhead. "that all of them may be one, Father, just as you are in me and I am in you." How do we, a church made up of "every tribe and tongue and nation" of the earth (Revelation 13:7, MEV), achieve this level of unity? Only through the unity of faith in and obedience to the Word of God. Culture divides us while God's truth defines us. We are called to let the Word of God define our unity while our various cultures describe our diversity.

This concept of unity with diversity must be the ruling sentiment of our public worship. Each of us must express our love for the Lord in our unique styles while respecting the culture of other worshipers in our family. This was the exact work of the disciples as they left Israel and went into all the world with the Gospel of Christ.

> *For he himself is our peace, who has made the two groups one and has destroyed the barrier, the dividing wall of hostility, by setting aside in his flesh the law with its commands and regulations. His purpose was to create in himself one new humanity out of the two, thus making peace, and in one body to reconcile both of them to God through the cross, by which he put to death their hostility. He came and preached peace to you who were far away and peace to those who were near. For through him we both have access to the Father by one Spirit. ...This mystery is that through the gospel the Gentiles are heirs together with Israel, members together of one body, and sharers together in the promise in Christ Jesus. (Ephesians 2:14–18; 3:6)*

> *But you are a chosen people, a royal priesthood, a holy nation, God's special possession, that you may declare the praises of him who called you out of darkness into his wonderful light. Once you were not a people, but now you are the people of God; once you had not received mercy, but now you have received mercy. (1 Peter 2:9–10)*

The most visible, powerful, and transformational way to be ONE in Jesus is through worship in unity with diversity. The church must be a transformed body fully informed by Scripture and fully alive in our culture. This is no easy task, as it demands skillful and sensitive leadership. It also demands a unified and fully informed congregation, which is the purpose of this little book. In these pages, we will explore the biblical truth on worship and the reasonable response we can give as the People of God.

What results from worship in unity with diversity? Worship, discipleship, fellowship, and evangelism will be the result, a church fully engaged in the call of God.

Fire and Form

The personal preference of some worshipers is for "on-fire" worship that is exciting, fun, and transformative. Let's call that kind of worship "Fire." At the same time, the tastes of other worshipers tend toward a predictable service full of order and transforming truth. We can call this "Form." Which is correct?

They both are correct. Personal preference (culture) would demand that we choose between the two, while a careful examination of the Bible reveals calls for both. Worship leaders operate in the dynamic center between opposite poles. The terms "Fire" and "Form" represent these polarities. Christianity was born in fire, but the Holy Spirit also moves in form. Finding our place on the line between these and other polarities is one of the great challenges of the ministry of worship. Let's take them in reverse order.

Form

Form is essential to Christian worship. If you say that Spirit-led worship is about freedom, you are correct. But it is a freedom within Scriptural limits and within the spiritual framework of the character of God and the ways of the Spirit. True worship is fire focused by form.

None of us wants an empty form. We long for worship services where people are healed and delivered, sinners are saved, believers are filled with the Spirit, and the Word of God is proclaimed in power. Shouldn't we, therefore, throw off all forms and let the Spirit have His way? We should let the Spirit have His way, but the Bible reveals God as a God of order and form. Before the Spirit moved upon the earth in creative power, the earth was "without form and void" (Genesis 1:2, ESV). After the move of the Spirit, the earth came into order: day and night were organized, as were the lights in the sky, the sea, and the dry land, as well as the life in the sea, on the land, and flying through the skies.

Creation tells us of an orderly and powerful Creator-God. He fashioned Adam from the earth, creating the human form. Then He breathed the breath of life into Adam and lit the fire known as the human spirit. Today, as we worship, that human spirit within connects with the Spirit of God and "we cry 'Abba, Father'" (Romans 8:17)! God breathes life into us as we worship.

Fire

Wherever you may read this, the fire of the Spirit is available to you. It is not American, this fire, or Asian, or African, nor does it belong to any other race or culture of man. It is not Baptist, Pentecostal, Liturgical, or Evangelical. The fire of the Holy Spirit is the presence of the Lord.

- » As a star, this fire guided the wise men and lit the Bethlehem skies with angels.
- » It radiated from Jesus' eyes to the eyes of fishermen, and they forsook their nets to follow Him.
- » This fire scorched the hypocrisy of the religious leaders and chased the money changers from the Temple.
- » The flame may have flickered before Pilate but was bright enough for a beaten, exhausted Jesus to declare His Kingdom greater than Pilate's domain or even that of Caesar.
- » For a moment on the cross, the fiery eyes closed.
- » But a split-spirit-second later, Jesus strode the streets of hell with a fire in His belly hotter than perdition's flames. He wrested the keys of death, hell, and the grave from Satan.
- » Like a holy torch, His holiness led captivity captive as he freed the prisoners of faith. Three days later, the angel rolled the stone away to reveal an empty tomb.
- » When the women met Jesus, they soon felt the old fire again— He was alive!
- » The two believers on the Emmaus road felt the fire burning in their hearts as Jesus explained the Word to them.
- » The Disciples knew His fire again when they saw Him.
- » On the Day of Pentecost, tongues of fire sat upon each of the one hundred and twenty, fires of cleansing and healing, the fires of the presence of Jesus.

New Covenant Worship

This is our New Covenant worship—the fires of Spirit within the forms of truth. And this, chapter by chapter, will be our subject.

CHAPTER 1
FINDING THE BOOK AGAIN

Biblical Reformation Leads to Revival

> *Hilkiah the high priest said to Shaphan the secretary, "I have found the Book of the Law in the temple of the LORD." He gave it to Shaphan, who read it...When the king heard the words of the Book of the Law, he tore his robes. (2 Kings 22:8, 11)*

A Skillful Craftsman

The call for workers went out across the land from young King Josiah himself. The Temple needed repair. Skilled carpenters and stone masons answered the call, as did their young apprentices and unskilled day laborers. No one knows whether it was a master craftsman, a trainee, or just an ordinary guy, but somebody found the lost Books of the Law somewhere in the neglected and abused House of God. Imagine the excitement as news of the discovery worked its way up the chain of command:

- » From an excited worker vaguely sensing the importance of the dusty scrolls
- » to a skilled craftsman recognizing the quality of the workmanship of the manuscripts in the trembling hands of his helper,
- » to a priest, then to the high priest,
- » then to the secretary of state, and finally,
- » to the king himself.

They Found the Book, and They Read It.

The king tore his robes when the book was read in his presence. He realized more repair was needed than crumbling plaster, cracked walls, or leaking ceilings. The worship life of the people was in dire need of repair, reform, and restoration.

This King Josiah, who tore his robes, was twenty-six years old. He had taken the throne when he was only eight before he had learned the wicked ways of his fathers. Perhaps his mother is given special mention in the Bible because she instilled in the boy a different spirit than the spirit of his age. It may be that the boy had seen glimpses of principles brighter than the darkness of the rule of raw power at her hand. Maybe he had even known the sweetness of the presence of the Lord in his mother's touch.

At sixteen, he sought the God of his father, David. At age twenty, he began his campaign to purify the nation of the heinous idolatry that gripped the people of God. When the Book of the Law was found and read to him, he commanded that it be read throughout the land, and reforms, based on demands of Scripture, marked his reign. He conducted a worship reformation unparalleled in the history of Israel and Judah.

Constant Worship Reform

I harbor no pretense of royalty—I'm no king; I'm just a worship leader, but I do, however, identify with young Josiah.

- » I came to know Jesus in my mother's Sunday school class when I was a child. I learned to sing songs like *Jesus Loves Me This I Know.*
- » I remember a picture on the wall of Jesus, the Good Shepherd, carrying a poor, injured lamb on his broad shoulders. I sensed the very presence of the Good Shepherd in that little Sunday school room as my Mother's sweet alto voice led us in song.
- » We were singing, *Oh, How I Love Jesus,* and I knew somehow that I was that little injured lamb and that Jesus had me in His strong arms.

As a doubting teen, I tested but could not dismiss what I had seen and heard, and as an adult, these simple truths have been my compass as the winds of fads and traditions have challenged my ministry.

- » I want to lead people to know the love of Jesus because the Bible is true and speaks to them.
- » I want to help them love Jesus because he first loved them.
- » I want them to realize that no matter their injury's severity, His broad shoulders are safe.

And I am a reformer.

The worship conditions handed to young King Josiah were far worse than any I have seen. The account of his reforms in 2 Kings 23 paints the lurid picture of the worship handed down to him by his fathers.

- » The Temple of Jehovah was host to the worship of Baal and Asherah, male and female deities of the Canaanites.
- » Male prostitutes were housed in the Temple area, and
- » skillful women wove garments to use in the worship of "Baal and Asherah and all the starry hosts" (2 Kings 23:4).
- » The countryside and villages had also fallen to unimaginable paganism.

High places, shrines, and altars marred the land, but Josiah destroyed them and the unholy priests who manned them.

I doubt things are that bad at your church; I know they aren't at mine! But a worship leader is a reformer wherever he or she is serving.

Semper Reformanda!—Always Reforming

One principle of the Reformation is *Semper Reformanda!,* or "always reforming." We must be vigilant to see that the Book of God doesn't get lost in the House of God. We are the carpenters, stonemasons, apprentices, and laborers who have answered the call to restore the House of God, the New Testament Temple, the Church, and the "Habitation of God by His Spirit" (Ephesians 2:19–22).

- » Are we more skilled in our traditions than in the ways of the Book?
- » Has the Book been lost in our house?

As Reformers, we must constantly seek the face of God, the will of God, and the plan of God so that the worship we lead will be an encounter with God. God's face, His will, and His plan are found in His Book.

Should we settle for a version of Christian worship that doesn't read like the Book?

- » Where are the miracles, signs, and wonders?
- » Where is the community of the Redeemed?
- » Where is the Kingdom of God come to earth?

- » Where is the form of godliness that throbs with the Power of God?
- » Where is the conviction of the Holy Spirit that grips the souls of sinners?
- » Where is the River of Life that flows from the Throne of God to the healing of the nations?

Have we lost the Book of God in the House of God?

- » Are we still a holy counterculture, loving the lost with selfless love, while calling the nation to repentance and the church to holiness?
- » Can the Book be found on the pulpit, or have other books shunted it aside?
- » Do we sing the book or sentimental, nostalgic artifacts or transient, trivial, narcissistic anthems to ourselves?

We are workmen who have been called by the King. Let us put on our work clothes.

- » Let us find our work gloves and our tools.
- » Let us search the Temple for the Book.
- » Like the King, let us tear our robes in sorrow and repentance as the words of the Book stream over us in a healing stream. These lovely robes won't save us. They won't win us a visitation from the King.

Only the words of the Book will speak peace to us with a voice as tender as my mother's, "Oh, how I love Jesus because He first loved me."

The steps in the three-part process of worship renewal are these:

- » The biblical reformation of prayer and public worship is the first step. This goes deeper than reformation by popular trends or by copying the methods of others.
- » The personal renewal of spirituality begins with prayer and continues with righteous living.
- » The seeking of the revival of the fiery heart that powers an obedient and, therefore, victorious life.If these are your desires for your church, join me as we, in the words of the Prophet Isaiah, "tremble at His Word."

Chapter 1—Finding the Book Again

<u>For Class Discussion</u>

1. Discuss other sources of information about how worship should be done.

2. What does the Latin phrase, Semper Reformanda!, mean to you?

3. What other kinds of worship reformation besides biblical reformation have you observed?

4. How can the Word of God become lost in the House of God?

5. What does it mean for the church to be a holy counterculture?

CHAPTER 2
PRAISE AND WORSHIP

Understanding these Important Terms

Have you ever wondered why worship services tend to start with a fast song and end with a slow one?

This common practice is not one of personal choice or even of practicality. It is rooted in a deep understanding of how the Bible instructs us to enter the presence of the Lord. There is a protocol, a way it should be done. When we stop and think about this, it makes sense that the Scriptures would provide just such a pattern.

» Concerning public worship, the Bible says that "everything should be done in a fitting and orderly way" (1 Corinthians 14:40).

» In Romans, Paul exhorts us to present ourselves to God in a spiritual worship which is "reasonable," perhaps even "logical" would be a good translation (Romans 12:1).

The logical, reasonable, fitting, and orderly way is the truth behind the structure of New Covenant liturgy—"the work of the people" in worship.

To understand this, we must understand the words we are using, especially "praise and worship." These terms are not synonyms. Sometimes, we treat them as if they mean the same thing, but they do not. What does the internet say?

Praise:

Verb: express warm approval or admiration of. "We can't praise Chris enough—he did a brilliant job." Synonyms: commend, applaud, eulogize, compliment, congratulate, lionize, admire, hail, laud.

Noun: the expression of approval or admiration for someone or something. "The audience was full of praise for the whole production." Synonyms: approval, acclaim, admiration, approbation, acclamation, commendation.

Worship:

Noun: the feeling or expression of reverence and adoration for a deity. "the worship of God." Synonyms: reverence, veneration, adoration, glorification, glory, exaltation.

Verb: show reverence and adoration for (a deity); honor with religious rites. "The Maya built jungle pyramids to worship their gods." Synonyms: revere, reverence, venerate, pay homage, adore, praise, pray to, glorify, exalt, extol, in other words, *"Honor to Whom Honor Is Due."*

What is the primary distinction?

Both humans and God receive praise. The New Testament tells us repeatedly that we are to honor, a form of praise, those who are worthy.

> *Render therefore to all their due: taxes to whom taxes are due, customs to whom customs, fear to whom fear, honor to whom honor. (Romans 13:7, NKJV)*

Parents do well to praise their children and to let them hear the deserved recognition of others from the mouths of their parents.

On the other hand, only God is worthy of worship. The same Bible that instructs us to be generous with the praise of others warns us that there is only One God, and He alone is worthy of worship. In fact, God's status as supremely worthy serves as the engine of the magnificent and continuous praise and worship in the Throne Room of God. Our two earthly witnesses to the worship of heaven agree in the smallest of details of the worship before the Throne of God. Read about it in Isaiah 6 and Revelation 4–5. It is the supreme worthiness of God that will send every person ever made to their knees to confess that Jesus is Lord to the Glory of God the Father (Philippians 2:10).

The Importance of the Distinction

Understanding this distinction, let us define praise and worship in the light of His presence. Here are the characteristics of praise:

- » **Praise** is the expression of thanksgiving to the Lord and the exaltation of the Lord that brings us into His presence.
- » **Praise** is the willful entrance into the presence of God by speaking forth thanksgiving to God and by exalting His name, character, mighty deeds, and glory. **Praise** is a deliberate action of soul and body. We praise God by expressing gratitude to Him and by proclaiming His glory, deeds, and character.
- » **Praise** is centered on God but is often expressed to others. We tell others how thankful we are or how great God is.
- » **The music of praise** tends to be horizontal in direction, singing about God.

Now let us examine the characteristics of worship:

- » **Worship** is the expression of submission to God, adoration of Him, and commitment to Him.
- » **Worship** is the willing response of our spirit to the revelation of the character of God by the moving of His Spirit in our hearts.
- » **Worship** is the act of communing with God when we are in His presence. We worship God by expressing love for Him and commitment to Him.
- » **Worship** is centered on God himself and is primarily expressed directly to Him, although many worshipful expressions of God's glory can be directed to others.
- » **The music of worship** tends to be vertical in direction, singing directly to the Lord—in other words, songs of prayer. Through praise, we enter the Lord's presence. Through worship, we respond to His presence.

The Praise-to-Worship Sequence

Repeatedly, we are told in the Bible to enter the Lord's presence with praise and then to respond to His visitation with worship.

Scriptures about the Praise-to-Worship Sequence

SCRIPTURE	PRAISE	WORSHIP
Psalm 24:3, NKJV	Who may ascend into the hill of the Lord?	Or who many stand in His holy place?
Psalm 29:1–2, NKJV	Give unto the Lord, O you mighty ones, Give unto the Lord glory and strength. Give unto the Lord the glory due His name;	Worship the Lord in the beauty of holiness.
Psalm 99:5, 9, NKJV	Exalt the Lord our God	And worship at His footstool—He *is* holy.
	Exalt the Lord our God	And Worship at His holy hill…
Psalm 100:1–5, NKJV	Make a joyful shout to the Lord, all you lands! Serve the Lord with gladness; Come before His presence with singing. Enter into His gates with thanksgiving, *And* into His courts with praise. Be thankful to Him, *and* bless His name.	Know that the Lord, He *is* God; *It is* He *who* has made us, and not we ourselves; *We are* His people and the sheep of His pasture. For the Lord *is* good; His mercy *is* everlasting. And His truth *endures* to all generations.
James 4:8a, NKJV	Draw near to God	And He will draw near to you.

This establishes a two-part process of praise leading to worship. Here is what happens:

1. As the people of God minister to the Lord with thanksgiving and exaltation and exhort one another to join in praising God, the Lord responds with the two-fold gift of His presence and His sovereignty (Psalm 22:3).

2. When the Lord grants worshipers a deep sense of His Manifest presence, we respond with worship: adoration, devotion, commitment, and communing with Him.

This illustration describes this reasonable praise-to-worship sequence.

This is a key to understanding how worship is planned and led. Of course, the great biblical illustration of this is the Tabernacle/Temple Model. It is the Old Covenant illustration of our New Covenant reality.

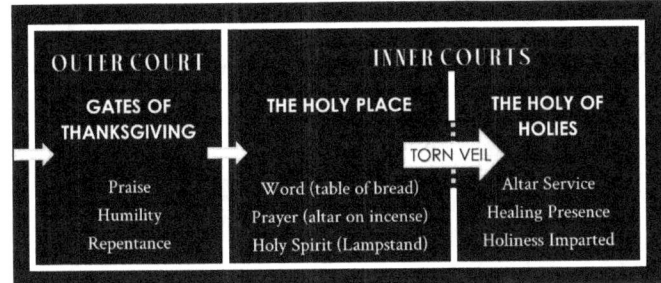

The Classical Pentecostal worship structure conforms to this biblical pattern. So, there is more going on than fast songs and slow songs, or as I heard one pastor describe, "happy songs and sad songs." When the worship service starts with a lively song of Thanksgiving, it isn't a cultural thing; it is the entrance to the manifest presence of God. As Isaiah said, "Go through the gates!"

Go through, Go through the gates! Prepare the way for the people; Build up, Build up the highway! Take out the stones, lift up a banner for the peoples! (Isaiah 62:10, NKJV)

For more on this topic, go to: "Recovering the Wilderness Protocol"

https://stevephifer.com/recovering-the-wilderness-protocol/

For Class Discussion

1. Describe in your own words the differences between praise and worship.
2. Discuss the validity of The-Praise-Leads-to-Worship sequence in the structure of the worship service.
3. What are some common characteristics of songs of praise?
4. What are some common characteristics of songs of worship?
5. What has been your experience of the Pentecostal Worship Structure: Worship/Word/Altar?

CHAPTER 3
PRIVATE WORSHIP, PUBLIC WORSHIP, AND THE PRESENCE OF GOD

Private/Public Worship

True Worship is always personal. Sometimes, we worship in the company of others in the community of the redeemed, and sometimes, we worship privately in the Secret Place. Both venues are vital to the Christian life. Their relationship is crucial to good worship theology and effective worship practice. True effectiveness as a believer in the Lord Jesus begins and is maintained in the Secret Place of prayer. Jesus gives us important details on private worship and how it fuels the public life of devotion to God. Paul tells us about the Life of Prayer that leads to a powerful public ministry. Of course, the Bible is also our source of information about public worship. There is so much to know, so much to teach.

Private Worship

For most of my ministry life, the emphasis has been on public worship—what we sing, say, and do in church. My shameful little secret has been that I struggled with private worship. I don't think I am alone in this struggle. The Scriptures and church history demonstrate the vital linkage between private prayer and public worship. In the next two chapters, I will present a brief exposition of the teachings of Jesus and the Apostles on private prayer. For now, let me emphasize private prayer's role in public worship. In essence, private worship fuels public worship. Paul said it this way:

> *What then shall we say, brothers and sisters? When you come together, each of you has a hymn, or a word of instruction, a revelation, a tongue or an interpretation. Everything must be done so that the church may be built up (1 Corinthians 14:26).*

It is apparent that these people were spending time with Jesus in the Secret Place. They came to church ready to worship because they had been worshiping all week! All the Apostle did was give them form for their fire—"for the strengthening of the church."

Is there anything more affirming in the believer's life than this: to hear from the Lord in the Secret place through the week and then hear the worship leader and pastor present those same truths in the public worship service? The Holy Spirit is speaking to the church.

> *Whoever has ears, let them hear what the Spirit says to the churches (Revelation 3:22).*

This hearing of the voice of the Spirit is our privilege as New Covenant believers.

Public Worship

We are meant to serve the Lord in community, not just on our own. Corporate Biblical images abound:

- » the army of the Lord,
- » the Body of Christ,
- » a Holy Nation,
- » a Holy-Royal Priesthood,
- » a People Purchased by God, and several more.

There are no lone-wolf Christians. Corporate worship includes corporate prayer, one of the most powerful forces in all of creation. It is also a public witness to the claims of Christ. Our praise proclaims Him Lord and Savior, Healer and Baptizer, ever-present Friend, and soon-coming King! The Blessed Sacrament of The Lord's Table celebrates the whole salvation narrative: the creation, the incarnation, the atonement, the resurrection, the coming of the Holy Spirit, the Lordship of Christ, and His soon return. True worship is one of the most evangelistic things the church can do!

Worship and Time

At the heart of private and public worship is the concept of Sacred Time. We are told to redeem the time. How do we do that? One way is to honor the Lord with our calendars and clocks. Private worship is an attempt to live the Life of Prayer. We can "pray without ceasing" with daily prayer and Bible reading. In ancient spirituality, the minimum daily prayer was morning and evening. To start and end each day with prayer, with private worship, is to frame each day in worship.

The weekly expression of Sacred Time is the Lord's Day. The Lord's Day is more than the Jewish Sabbath, a day of worship and rest. The Christian Lord's Day is the Sabbath plus a celebration of Jesus! The first day of the week is really the eighth day of creation—the day of the New Creation—the Day of the Resurrection! Christians worship, rest, and celebrate the Jesus story—the Gospel of Christ, which is the power of God unto salvation for all peoples (Romans 1:16).

So, we worship Him daily and gather weekly to celebrate the Lord. Private worship and public worship are each vital to the other and essential for the church today.

Understanding the Presence of God

How can we enter the presence of Someone Who is everywhere?

I want to do all I can to prompt personal worship of the Lord Jesus. The answers to questions like the one above will help. True Worship ranges far beyond the sanctuary to the home altar, the place of personal worship, and even the workplace. Worship is a vital part of Life. As people say today, it is 24-7!

Worship is so much larger than denominational, traditional, or personal preferences. To quote Scripture, worship is the "path of life."

> *You make known to me the path of life; you will fill me with joy in your presence, with eternal pleasures at your right hand. (Psalm 16:11).*

"With joy in your presence," the Psalmist says. This brings us back to our question: How can we enter the presence of Someone Who is everywhere? The Bible indicates that there are three characteristics of God's presence:

1. omnipresence,
2. inward presence, and
3. manifest presence.

The omnipresence of the Lord means He is everywhere at all times, demonstrating His absolute mastery of time and space, which are, after all, His creations. Paul preached God's omnipresence to the Greeks at Mars Hill (Acts.17:28). It is the most general revelation of God's presence.

The inward presence of the Lord is His presence within the hearts and lives of His people. Throughout the Bible, God speaks of dwelling with and in His people. For example:

> ...For we are the temple of the living God. As God has said: "I will live with them and walk among them, and I will be their God, and they will be my people" (2 Corinthians 6:16).

The manifest presence of the Lord is deeper still. God is present within creation, within His people, and *within in the praise of His people*. The Lord inhabits, or dwells in, the praises of His people. Modern translations also say that He is enthroned upon the praise of His people.

> But thou art holy, O thou that inhabitest the praises of Israel (Psalm 22:3, ASV).

> Yet thou art holy, enthroned upon the praises of Israel (Psalm 22:3, RSV).

When God's people express their praise (thanksgiving and exaltation) to God, **He responds!** He shares with them a deeper sense of His presence.

How does this happen? How does the Lord intensify our awareness of His presence? Jesus gives us the answer when we listen to His conversation with Nicodemus (John 3:5).

- Jesus said that the Spirit of God moves like the wind, unseen and mysterious, yet powerfully obvious in effect.
- Like the air around us, the unseen omnipresence of God surrounds us and gives us life.

We may not be aware of His presence, but just as we would miss the air, we would be desperate if His omnipresence were suddenly taken from us.

Still, we go on, taking the omnipresence of God for granted as we do the earth's atmosphere, giving it little thought. But when the air stirs, we notice.

> A cool breeze refreshes, and a mighty wind impresses.

When we turn our hearts toward God to be His people, He begins to move in our hearts, like air beginning to stir. This is His inward presence. And when we praise Him, He moves within us like a mighty wind, powerful in its effect, and we experience His manifest presence.

So, praise Him and feel the wind!

This can happen for us privately and publicly, but only when we turn our whole hearts toward Him and forget about everybody else! Worship is the atmosphere of Heaven. Come before His Presence.

Praise Him; worship Him and breathe the air!

For Class Discussion

1. Describe in your own words the relationship between private worship of the individual and the public worship of the church.
2. Choose one of the five biblical images of the church and describe its relationship to you. (the army of the Lord, the Body of Christ, a Holy Nation, a Holy-Royal Priesthood, a People Purchased by God)
3. Discuss the concept of Sacred Time and its relationship to private and public worship.
4. Discuss this statement from the text: "How can we enter the presence of Someone Who is everywhere?"
5. Discuss the three dimensions of the Lord's presence and their relationship to private and public worship.

Stephen Phifer—*The Wonder of Worship*

CHAPTER 4
TWO LENSES REQUIRED

Understanding Worship in Spirit and Truth

Yet a time is coming and has now come when the true worshipers will worship the Father in the Spirit and in truth, for they are the kind of worshipers the Father seeks. God is spirit, and his worshipers must worship in the Spirit and in truth (John 4:23–24).

The Right and Left of It

For those who wear glasses or contact lenses, the difference between the left and right lenses is clear to see (pun intended). The left lens cannot serve the right eye and vice versa. Also, having only one lens is just as bad as not having any glasses at all. These words of Jesus to the woman at the well challenge us. I have heard noted preachers stumble as they try to explain what Jesus meant by "spirit and truth." While there is certainly no final word on what this statement means, let me share what I see in these incredible words. Let's refer to Strong's:

> "worship"—NT:4352 *proskuneo*- meaning to kiss, to fawn or to prostrate oneself in homage (do reverence to, adore)[2] "spirit"—NT:4151 *pneuma*- a current of air, i.e., breath or a breeze; figuratively, a spirit, i.e. (human) the rational soul, mental disposition, etc., or an angel, demon, or (divine) God, Christ's spirit, the Holy Spirit[3] "truth"—NT:225 *aletheia* truth[4]

According to Strong, worship means worship, spirit means spirit, and truth means truth. Where does that leave us? With no hidden meanings

---
[2] Strong, James. "G4352 – *proskuneo*." *The New Strong's Expanded Exhaustive Concordance of the Bible.* Red letter ed. Nashville, TN: Thomas Nelson, 2010.
[3] Strong, James. "G602 – *pneuma*." *The New Strong's Expanded Exhaustive Concordance of the Bible.* Red letter ed. Nashville, TN: Thomas Nelson, 2010.
[4] Strong, James. "G602 – *aletheia*." *The New Strong's Expanded Exhaustive Concordance of the Bible.* Red letter ed. Nashville, TN: Thomas Nelson, 2010.

in the Greek, let's take a different approach and ask questions of the text. Whose spirit? What truth?

Whose spirit is involved in the worship the Father seeks?

Simply put: ours and His. To worship in a way that pleases God, we must worship from the depths of our human spirit.

- » This "homage, reverence, and adoration" is not surface but springs like a well from deep within us.
- » It isn't perfunctory or automatic but requires full energy, focus, and concentration.
- » It is an exercise of the whole person, body, soul, and spirit.

Also, this worship is directed by and empowered by God's Spirit. The goals of the Holy Spirit are the goals of the worshiper, as are the motivations and the methods.

What truth does this worship demand?—our truth and God's truth.

Worship in truth is a single-hearted, hot-hearted enterprise. Although benefits flow from the relationship with God expressed by worship, we do not worship to get the benefits.

- » True Worship is not a self-improvement plan, a church-growth tool, or a marketing ploy.
- » It springs from a pure heart and a "poor" heart, as Jesus said in the Sermon on the Mount (Matthew 5): a humble spirit, a heart set "on things above," not things below (Colossians 3:1).
- » Also, true worship is expressed in biblical terms, methods, and patterns. True worship is defined by the truth of God, not by the surrounding culture.

The challenge of worshiping in the Kingdom's truth while living in the world's culture has faced every church in every land in every age of Christianity. Eternal, changeless truths must be expressed and experienced by worshipers in current, relevant languages and methods.

Incarnation

This is the incarnation process—bringing heaven's exalted truth into a bit of fallen humanity here on earth. In this way, worship in truth transcends culture, speaking universals within localities—the Word made flesh and dwelling among us as we worship.

So, we worship from our spirits as we are led by the Holy Spirit, and we worship in total sincerity as we are informed and shaped by the truth of the Word of God—worship in spirit and in truth.

Two Lenses to See Clearly

These are the two necessary lenses through which we must view our personal and corporate worship.

- » By nature, some of us lean toward the "spirit" side of worship. "Spirit-people," as I call them, welcome change and innovation, and they love new songs, new forms, and free-flowing, spontaneous worship.

- » Others are who we might call "truth-people." They resist change, suspect innovation, don't care for new songs or forms of worship and prefer that things be predictable and comforting.

To sort this out, we must remember the context of Jesus' statement: a culture clash over worship methodology and location. "Some say we should worship in this mountain and others say in that temple. What do you say, Jesus?"

He said, in effect, we should not limit our worship to our personal preferences however we gained them. If by nature or culture we prefer "spirit-things" or "truth-things," the God we worship is bigger than any of those things. True worship will stretch us beyond our comfort zones, beyond our personalities, and beyond our cultural preferences. Why?—because true worship is based on Who God is, not who we are.

> *God is spirit, and his worshipers must worship in the Spirit and in truth (John 4:24).*

So, by faith let us put on both lenses.

We should look at each passage of Scripture and examine each service, song, or ceremony with both lenses in place. To get a true stereo image, an in-depth, full-dimensioned image of how we interact with the Lord Jesus, we must evaluate our personal and corporate worship philosophy and practice from both vantage points. We must worship from our spirits as we are led by His Spirit, and we must do so in deepest sincerity, with no hidden motives, and in obedience to the truth of the Word of God.

We will be amazed as our vision clears with both lenses in place.

For Class Discussion

1. How is New Covenant Worship (in Spirit and Truth) different from Old Covenant Worship (In time and place)
2. Explain these words of Jesus: "they are the kind of worshipers the Father seeks" (John 4:23).
3. Whose spirit and truth does the command to worship in spirit and truth involve? Ours? God's? Both?
4. How does the concept of Incarnation, the process of the Word becoming flesh, enter into our understanding of worship?
5. What is meant by "Two Lenses to See Clearly?"

CHAPTER 5
DYNAMICS OF SPIRIT

The Three Principles

When the Advocate comes, whom I will send to you from the Father—the Spirit of truth who goes out from the Father—he will testify about me (John 15:26).

What then shall we say, brothers and sisters? When you come together, each of you has a hymn, or a word of instruction, a revelation, a tongue or an interpretation. Everything must be done so that the church may be built up... Therefore, my brothers and sisters, be eager to prophesy, and do not forbid speaking in tongues. But everything should be done in a fitting and orderly way (1 Corinthians 14:26, 39–40).

Fundamentals of Life

Fundamentals often come in sets of three:
- » time (past, present, and future),
- » matter (solid, liquid, and gas),
- » music (melody, harmony, and rhythm),
- » the spiritual life (faith, hope, and love),
- » Pentecostal worship (worship, word, and altar), and
- » worship renewal (theology, doxology, and spirituality).

The fundamental ways of the Spirit of God in worship are also threefold:

1. The Holy Spirit's ministry is Christ-centered.
2. He seeks to edify the whole church, and
3. He moves in fitting and orderly ways.

These three dynamics are the absolutes. Every worship service will have these characteristics in a wonderful, three-fold dynamism. The methods we use will vary from event to event. The music will change, and the order will adapt to the shifting emphases of the Spirit, but these three forces will always be in effect.

Worship services should always be centered on Jesus. The people must always enter the voluntary disciplines of public worship—that is, to worship with a sensitivity to the whole congregation. Finally, the Holy Spirit always moves in a fitting and orderly manner. Let's take a closer look at each of these dynamics.

Christ-centered Worship

This dynamic is the key to the other two. A "fitting and orderly" service that isn't about Jesus is not a worship service. An event that helps the members of the congregation without lifting up Jesus as the Savior, Healer, Baptizer, Deliverer, Redeemer, and Soon-coming King is just a self-help seminar, not a worship service. It is so easy to place someone or something else at the center. It may be the music or the musicians, the worship tradition, the worship leaders, or even the desires of the congregation or those of the community, but each church is in constant danger of having another center other than the Lord Himself.

- » If tradition is at the center instead of Jesus, a church can become a museum.
- » If the singers and instrumentalists are at the center, the church becomes a performing arts center.
- » If the preacher is at the center, the church becomes a cult of personality.

The Holy Spirit has no interest in supporting any of these institutions. His goal is to reveal Jesus to us and shape our hearts to receive from Him.

Market-driven Worship

It follows that if the desires of Jesus are not foremost in our minds, the desires of someone else are. Worship that isn't Christ-centered becomes market-driven. We fall into the enemy's trap. Satan wants to divide us in a thousand different ways: culture, race, generation, social status, musical tastes, lifestyle, and even fashion sense, just to name a few. When we "target" a group of people—"we want those people here," we are inevitably excluding others—"we don't want those people." Paul told the Ephesian church that Jesus had come to tear down the walls of hostility between the cultures. When we deliberately place Him at the center of our worship, He does exactly that.

We must beware of church growth plans that strengthen and decorate walls that Jesus wants to tear down.

Jesus unites worshipers across any line Satan or man himself can draw. He is the only one who can bring the races, cultures, economic classes, and generations together. So, the first goal of the Holy Spirit in public worship is to keep Jesus in the center.

The Strengthening of the Church

Private worship and public worship are two complementary but different things. While both involve "spirit and truth" and the ministry of the Holy Spirit we are discussing in this chapter, public worship includes the discipline of being "in the congregation." Things are different when we are gathered together with the saints of God. We need to agree together, encourage one another, pray for each other, and bear one another's burdens. We need to share our joys and sorrows together as a community of faith. The second goal of the Holy Spirit in public worship is to build this community of faith on Jesus—the household of faith—on Christ the Cornerstone, to use a biblical image. This means that worship leaders must get into the flow of the Holy Spirit both as they plan the service and as they lead it.

God is the master of time.

He has no problem letting the worship leader know in advance what He wants to do in a particular service. The preacher needs to get a word from the Lord, and the worship music leader does as well. Then, in the service, worshipers must exercise personal discipline as they worship so that they do not distract from the ministry of the Holy Spirit to the whole body. In the secret place, we are free to do whatever we feel led to do in worship, but in the congregation, we need to consider our brothers and sisters in the Lord.

While the Lord deals with each worshiper, He is also moving the congregation forward in faith. Only when we march forth together are we really a mighty army. When this critical difference between private and public worship is seen by all, the church can avoid internal conflicts as we get our marching orders from the Captain of the Hosts.

A Fitting and Orderly Way

The third dynamic of the Spirit of God reflects God's very nature. God is the author of order and beauty and of form and function in perfect synthesis. If there is chaos in our worship, we have authored it, not the Lord. If our worship service is a series of random songs, prayers, speeches, and events, it reflects our nature, not God's nature. In the Corinthian instruction, Paul gives an astounding array of things we might do in worship. He commends the people on their full hearts, hearts filled, no doubt, by daily worship in the secret place. And he tells them to share what they have, but only as the Spirit leads.

The "fitting and orderly" way can be sensed by worship leaders ahead of time in worship planning, and it should be sensed by all the worshipers in the service itself. Pentecostal worship has a grass-roots quality to it. As Pastor James said in his letter to the churches at the Jerusalem conference, "For it seemed good to the Holy Spirit, and to us..." (Acts 15:28). When we get it right, everyone knows it. When we get it wrong, most know it as well. Once, after an altar service where someone had misused the gifts of the Spirit, my teenage daughter asked me, "Dad, why do we allow people to do that?" I told her that the freedom to get it right included the danger of someone getting it wrong, but it was worth it.

So, we are free to worship as the Spirit leads.

We are not free to worship any way we choose. He always has three goals in dynamic action: He wants to exalt the Lord Jesus, edify the church, and move decently and in order. Methods may change, music may come in or out of fashion, and technology may assist us in exciting new ways, but these three things are the essentials, the elements of worship, like matter, time, music, spirituality, and even God Himself—three who are really one.

For Class Discussion

1. Discuss the relationships among the three principles set forth in the three passages of Scripture at the beginning of this chapter:

    » The Holy Spirit exalts Jesus.

    » The Holy Spirit seeks to edify the church.

    » The Holy Spirit moves decently and in order.

2. What are the characteristics of Christ-centered worship?

3. How is Christ-centered worship different from market-driven worship?

4. How does public worship strengthen the church?

5. Explain the dynamics of worship that is done "decently and in order." Other translations say, in a "fitting and orderly way."

CHAPTER 6

DYNAMICS OF TRUTH

The Biblical Directives

*I will consider all your works and **meditate on** all your mighty deeds (Psalm 77:12, emphasis mine).*

*I will praise you with the harp for your faithfulness, my God; I will sing praise to you with the lyre, Holy One of Israel. **My lips will shout for joy when I sing praise to you**—I, whom you have delivered. My tongue will tell of your righteous acts all day long, for those who wanted to harm me have been put to shame and confusion (Psalm 71:22–24, emphasis mine).*

*Praise the LORD. Sing to the LORD a new song, his praise in the assembly of his faithful people. Let Israel rejoice in their Maker; let the people of Zion be glad in their King. **Let them praise his name with dancing and make music to him with timbrel and harp.** For the LORD takes delight in his people; he crowns the humble with victory (Psalm 149:1–4, emphasis mine).*

Absolutes and Variables

Just as we find three absolutes in the ways of the Holy Spirit (He always moves to exalt the Lord Jesus, edify the church, and He moves in a fitting and orderly way), we also find three types of biblical directives telling us what to do in worship: inner directives tell us how to think, vocal directives tell us how to speak, and physical directives tell us what to do. These are the absolutes. We might also call them principles or even directives. There are also relative truths employed by the Spirit and by us in the service of the unchanging absolutes, the principles. While the principles are always present as the Spirit leads us in worship, the directives will come and go depending on the leadership of the Spirit for a given service. If we treat a relative truth like an absolute truth, we are in error. That is how churches split over modes of worship, always a senseless and needless tragedy. Study this illustration of the principles and the directives.

The following is a section from my book, *Worship That Pleases God: The Passion and Reason of True Worship.*[5]

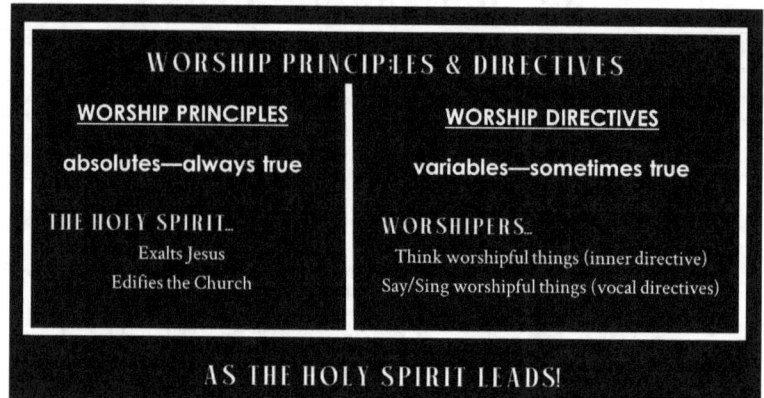

Biblical Directives for Worship

Directives are found in several forms in the Bible, direct commands, testimonies of true worshipers, and historical records of worshipers who pleased God. There are three types:

> - inward expression, vocal expression, and
> - physical expression. Since worship must be an outward expression flowing from the heart let us begin with the directives toward inward expression.

---

5 Phifer, Stephen R. *Worship that Pleases God, The Passion and Reason of True Worship.* Trafford Publishing, 2004, 2014.

Inward Expression Table

DIRECTIVE	PSALM REFERENCE[6]
Behold the Lord	27:4
Commune with the Lord (or one's heart)	4:4
Consider the Lord (His works)	8:3
Contemplate Him	119:15
Delight in Him	37:4
Desire Him (or His ways, or house)	27:4
Hope in the Lord	31:24
Inquire of the Lord	27:4
Know the Lord	100:3
Long for God	63:1
Meditate on His law, or deeds	1:2
Rest in Him	36:7
"See" Him	97:6
Seek Him	22:26
"Taste" that He is good	34:8
Trust in Him (most frequent directive)	118:8, 9

Authentic inward expression is essential to true worship. Jesus said that the passions of the heart will come pouring out of the mouth:

> *You brood of vipers, how can you who are evil say anything good? For the mouth speaks what the heart is full of (Matthew 12:34).*

These immeasurable directives will become obvious in our worship. Worship, and especially worship leading, reveals the contents of the heart. When people get upset about worship, or when a worship leader gets frustrated, it is important to listen carefully to what they say. What are the real issues: musical things or spiritual things? What attitude is presented, a humble, Christ-like spirit or prideful, critical spirit? Proper inward expressions and attitudes of worship will lead to the proper vocal expressions of worship. Lack of these internals will weaken and destroy the worship experience.

---

[6] References from the book of Psalms are most frequent and are cited only as chapter and verse.

Vocal Expression Table

DIRECTIVE	PSALM OR OTHER REFERENCE
Be silent	Habakkuk 2:20
Bless the Lord	103:1
Call upon God	17:6
Corporate praise	22:22
Corporate prayer	Acts 4:31
Corporate worship	95:6
Cry unto the Lord	3:4
Declare His name, glory, deeds,	118:17
Exalt His name, deeds,	34:3
Extol His virtue	30:1
Give thanks	18:49
Glorify Him	22:23
Magnify the Lord	34:3
Play musical instruments	150
Praise the Lord	150
Pray with understanding and with Spirit	1 Corinthians 14:15
Proclaim His Glory, deeds, name	96:2
Rejoice in the Lord	2:11
Shout unto the Lord	5:11
Sing with understanding and with spirit	1 Corinthians 14:15

Some of these modes of expression run afoul of Western sensibilities. That should not be surprising since the Bible is not a Western book. People in or from different cultures express themselves in decidedly different ways. Culture defines how people express emotion publicly. Northern European cultures are generally reserved and do not esteem the public display of emotion. Mediterranean, Latin, and African cultures express emotion very freely in public. Sincere worshipers whose sensitivities have been forged in the fires of a reserved culture are going to have difficulty with public praying, crying out to God, shouting, rejoicing, and so forth. At the same time, sincere worshipers from warmer climates will take to these public expressions readily. While all this is interesting and important to note, none of it changes what the Bible has to say. All of these methods of expression are biblical, whether we are comfortable with them or not. That does not mean that there are no controls or mechanisms to regulate when such expressions are proper. We will reason them out in relation to the principles. Keeping these sensibility problems in mind helps us approach the next category of directives.

The Scriptures do not overlook our physical activity while these inward expressions abide within us and while we vocalize our praise.

Physical Expression Table

DIRECTIVE	PSALM OR OTHER REFERENCE
Be still	4:4
Bow before Him	22:29
Clap our hands	47:1
Come before Him (His Presence)	65:2
Dance before Him	150
Enter His gates	100:4
Fall prostrate before Him	72:11
Fast unto God	Isaiah 58; Matthew 5–7 (Sermon on the Mount); Acts 13:1, 2
Kneel before Him	95
Lift our hands unto Him	8:2
Lift up our heads	24:7, 9
Look up to Him	5:3
Offer unto Him	119:108
Process before Him (the Processional)	68:24–25
Rest in Him	16:9
Sacrifice unto Him	107:22
Stand before Him	134:1
Tremble before Him	96:9

This list is not exhaustive, but it is amazing. Each of us, and certainly each domination or tradition, is tempted to add footnotes and explanations.

- » "We do not stand very long."
- » "We don't dance in our church."
- » "We don't lift our hands."
- » "We don't like banners."
- » "We don't believe people should fall down."
- » "We don't do processions."

There is great potential for confusion in these contradictory commands. Let us look carefully at this clash of traditions, remembering the woman at the well (John 4). She presented the Lord with a clash of traditions. Surely the answer is still the same—get things on a spiritual level, find out what the Father wants, and put His desires first. How do we know when to be silent and when to shout? Or how can we know when to be still and when to process, or when to stand and when to bow? How do we know when to consider the Lord's goodness or when to inquire in His temple? How do we avoid worshiping in the ways that feel natural to us at the expense of things we would rather not do? Is this a biblical menu where we choose the things we like to do and leave the rest alone? Have we elevated our feelings and traditions to the level of biblical authority? It is evident we need more than biblical directives to guide us in our worship. The three ever-present principles become our guide and our criteria: Does this directive exalt the Lord Jesus and edify the Body of Christ, and is it done in a fitting and orderly way?

Some may wonder if such a preponderance of Old Testament verses can really be taken as a set of directives for New Testament worship. This is a legitimate concern. Here is my reasoning from *Worship that Pleases God*:

> *Is this an imposition of Old Testament worship on New Testament believers? On the contrary, the New Testament commands us to use the Psalms—three times (Colossians 3:16, Ephesians 5:19, James 5:13). New Testament worshipers used the book of Psalms. It remains our textbook for worship that pleases God today. Is it not remarkable that there are so few references to animal sacrifices in the Psalms and so many, many references to spiritual sacrifices? This has been God's desire from the beginning.*[7]

So, like the Apostles and as leaders from every reformation movement in history have done, we learn about how to worship God under the New Covenant by use of the Book of Psalms as our guide.

The biblical principles of worship guide us in knowing what to do and when. There is no way I can overemphasize the importance of the difference between the directives and the principles. If we take only the

---

[7] Phifer, Stephen R. *Worship that Pleases God, The Passion and Reason of True Worship*. Trafford Publishing, 2004, 2014.

directives, our worship will be divisive and exclusive, engendering strife, but when we understand the principles behind the directives, we know how to let the Holy Spirit lead in worship that pleases God. Our worship will be unifying and inclusive, passionate and reasonable, bringing in His peace.

For Class Discussion

1. Discuss the variety and importance of the Inward Worship Directives.
2. Discuss the importance of the Vocal Worship Directives.
3. Discuss the proper modes of the Physical Worship Directives.
4. How do our various worship traditions affect these directives?
5. How does the Holy Spirit lead the church in the proper use of these many directives?

CHAPTER 7
BIBLICAL WORSHIP MUSIC

Psalms, Hymns, and Spiritual Songs

> *Do not get drunk on wine, which leads to debauchery. Instead, be filled with the Spirit, speaking to one another with **psalms, hymns, and songs from the Spirit**. Sing and make music from your heart to the Lord, always giving thanks to God the Father for everything, in the name of our Lord Jesus Christ (Ephesians 5:18–20, emphasis mine).*

> *Let the peace of Christ rule in your hearts, since as members of one body you were called to peace. And be thankful. Let the message of Christ dwell among you richly as you teach and admonish one another with all wisdom through **psalms, hymns, and songs from the Spirit**, singing to God with gratitude in your hearts. And whatever you do, whether in word or deed, do it all in the name of the Lord Jesus, giving thanks to God the Father through him (Colossians 3:15–17, emphasis mine).*

In contemporary spirituality, worship and music are too often thought of as synonymous. They are not. We have been together for several sessions now. This is Chapter 7, and only now are we talking about music. We won't even spend much time on the subject now, but it is important to get a trans-cultural, trans-generational, and trans-personal fix on what the Bible demands of our worship music. If you are not wondering how we can get such a view of worship, one that does not consider the cultural, generational, or personal preferences of people, you should be because this is not the normal approach to music. Music *is* culture, for heaven's sake!

Exactly.

Therefore, the Scriptures provide us with guiding truths in the realm of principles, not particulars. One of the most frequently made blunders we make concerning worship is to assume that the music that moves us should move everyone. We sometimes even act as if our preferences matched those of the Lord Jesus exactly or as if the Holy Spirit can only use the music that we can appreciate; effectively, we act as if the Father is only pleased by what pleases us. This monumentally arrogant supposition is too often found among the most sincere and otherwise humble people who are living for the Lord to the best of their ability and want with all their hearts to please Him.

It only makes sense that biblical demands of our music must be adaptable to all times and all cultures. The music of Western civilization has been in a state of evolution parallel to that of Western civilization itself. Simply put, most likely we would not recognize the musical language of King David as music at all. The actual sounds of the "psalms and hymns and spiritual songs" to which Paul refers would probably not please the contemporary Western musical ear. Like a scene from an early 1930s Cecil B. DeMille epic film where Cleopatra enters Rome to the strains of 19th-century music played on 20th-century orchestral instruments, we "hear" our music when we read the Bible. Our music is our music, nothing more and nothing less. It is not David's music or the apostle's music or that of the early church, the Middle Ages, or any other age of Western civilization. The same is true for Eastern music, African music, or island music that we need. These cultural expressions share very few elements. They are each the product of their own histories and evolutions. So, the meanings of these three key terms are not cultural, generational, or personal; they are theological. They refer not to the sound or form of the music but to its content and intent, to its text and its context.

Content and Intent

These two elements of song qualify the piece or disqualify it for use in worship.

> » Obviously, the content of worship music must be truth: the truth of God and the truth of man, God's revelation of Himself to us, and our response to that revelation. I often say that music is like a freight train; it moves powerfully down the tracks, and you can load many different things into it. As worship leaders, we need to freight our music with the Word of God and with sincere human heart-cries.

> But music is also always made with a purpose in mind, a specific work it is designed to do. Many times, a song itself may be loaded with truth, but the singer is not. He or she sings from a false motive, perhaps one of gaining attention or making an impression. This false intention on the part of the singer affects the usefulness of the music in the hands of the Holy Spirit. Can He exalt Jesus without lifting the performer up with pride?

The intent of the singer has hampered the song itself.

Text and Context

The text of the song, the words, form the heart of the song.

> Does the song express opinion, testimony, complaint, lament, praise, adoration, or petition, or does it promote emotionalism, nostalgia, sentiment, poor theology, or even untruth? These are important questions, and they are at the heart of the meanings of the three biblical terms we will examine in a moment. Also, is the text of the song expressed well by the musicality of the song? Musical language and textual language must support each other if the song is to hit its mark. This is much more complex than such simple-minded notions that slow music is sad and fast music is happy. It is the job of the songwriter to match the language of the music with the feeling of the meaning of the words. This is especially important for songs that are used in worship.

> Context is also important. Every song is presented after something and before something else. Each worship leader operates within the confines of a church family culture. These two things, the flow of the events of a service and the artistic/theological dimensions of the church body, determine the context in which a song is presented.

In short, we must have the right song for the right moment if our music is to be used by the Holy Spirit to exalt the Lord Jesus, edify the Body, and move decently and in order: Text and Context.

Psalms, Hymns, and Spiritual Songs

Now, let's unveil these mysteries. According to *Vine's Expository Dictionary of New Testament Words*,[8]

> » psalms are sacred songs with instrumental accompaniment.
> » Hymns are songs of praise addressed to God, and
> » spiritual songs are songs with a special touch of the Holy Spirit upon them.

I believe these definitions are as close as we can get to Paul's intentions when he wrote these parallel passages. We are much more familiar with the definitions we have substituted:

> » Psalms are Scripture's songs;hymns are old songs in books, andspiritual songs are the lively ones.It will be most helpful to examine the *biblical* meanings.

What Is a Psalm?

Psalms are more than just the book of Psalms, although these are certainly included. Psalms are sacred songs—songs set apart to God. We can find them anywhere, in Scripture or from composers, and in any style. The important thing is they are for God, and they are about God—sacred. Psalms are built on the pattern of the book of Psalms:

> » real and revealing of God's nature and man's heart and
> » proclamation of God's glory and life's enigmas; emotional and rational, repetitive and exhaustive, personal and congregational, joyful and sorrowful, a subject range that covers all of life.

Another important characteristic of biblical psalms is that they are designed to be accompanied by instruments—not recordings—instruments played by instrumentalists. Churches have become singer-centered, letting technology take the place of the instrumentalist. This is far from the heart of God. As Ephesians 5:19 says, "sing *and make music*" (NIV, emphasis mine). If we are to make our songs "sacred" by setting them apart to God, we must be flexible and able to follow the flow of the Holy Spirit. It takes living, breathing people to do that, instrumentalists and vocalists who are sensitive to the voice of God. Pastors, music pastors, and worship leaders

---

8 Vine, W.E.. *Vine's Expository Dictionary of New Testament Words: A Comprehensive Dictionary of the Original Greek Words with their Precise Meanings for English Reader.* MacDonald Publishing Co., 1989.

must take seriously the development of instrumentalists. The first type of biblical song, the psalm, demands it.

What is a Hymn?

What musical term is more controversial in the church today than "hymn." We can be sure that 50- to 100-year-old songs in a hardback book were *not* what Paul had in mind when he used the word "hymn." According to Vines, he meant songs of praise *addressed to God.* We have already established that psalms are songs of praise. The elevating difference about hymns is that they are addressed to God. According to these parallel passages, all our singing and music-making must be made *to God,* but hymns are *addressed* to Him. In other words, biblically, hymns are songs of prayer. There is a powerful dimension to a prayer that is sung by a congregation. When Jesus cleansed the Temple, he quoted Isaiah, saying that the Father's house would be a house of prayer for all nations (Matthew 21:13). The word Isaiah used was the Hebrew word for hymn. In other words, a mark of the house of God is that it is a place where prayers are sung. In the synagogue, prayers, usually from the Psalms, were chanted by the congregation.

This practice became a part of first-century Christian worship and has continued through the ages. As musical styles developed, songs of prayer developed as well. This is one of the common factors of the historic hymns written since the Reformation and the wonderfully diverse songs of the praise and worship movement, as well as the congregational songs of "modern" worship in the 21st Century. So many of the great songs are addressed to God, not to man; they are songs of prayer. Compare "My Jesus I Love Thee" with "I Love You, Lord" with "The Goodness of God." The musical differences reflect the hundred years or so of musical tradition that separates them. But the heart of each song is the same, and each song is addressed directly to God. This biblical understanding of hymns is essential to the process of bringing cultural and intergenerational peace to the church.

What is a Spiritual Song?

The power intensifies further with "spiritual songs." Sacred songs with instruments addressed to God can also be touched with the power of the Holy Spirit. The Spirit's power should be present on every psalm and hymn, so what is the need for another genre? To this point, the

Bible is instructing us in the use of composed songs. When worshipers improvise their own musical expressions of worship, the Holy Spirit can breathe through an entire congregation to create a symphony of worship unique to that moment and place. Many times, the gifts of the Spirit will flow in these moments, and the Lord speaks vital things to the fellowship. This level of worship requires a knowledgeable, skillful, and willing congregation. This does not happen by accident. It happens when the Holy Spirit opens the hearts of the singers and instrumentalists, who have a key role in releasing this song of the Lord and the hearts of the leaders and people to this ministry.

For more on spiritual songs, go to: https://stevephifer.com/spiritual-songs/.

And to: https://stevephifer.com/come-on-everybody-sing-part-one/

So there you have it, the great trans-cultural, trans-generational, trans-personal plan of God. Regardless of the musical language of certain people in a particular place and at a given time, the music God is listening for is full of truth, revelation, and mystery. It is about God, not about us. It is poured out willingly to the Lord as prayer from a sincere heart. Instruments accompany it, and at times, worshipers are released to improvise as the Spirit leads. Psalms, hymns, and spiritual songs are the universal repertoire of the universal church.

For Class Discussion

1. How do the qualities of content (what the song says) and the intent (what the song is intended to do in the service) qualify or disqualify a song for use in public worship?

2. How important are the text (the words of the song) and the context (the setting of the song) to its proper use in public worship?

3. Discuss the biblical definition of "psalm," contrasting it with our modern understanding.

4. Explore the differences between the biblical definition of "hymn" with our modern concept.

5. What is the biblical definition of "spiritual song," and what has been your experience of this type of worship singing?

CHAPTER 8

THE 7 BIBLICAL MODELS: 1 & 2

God's Dwelling Places: Altars

The Patriarchs built altars to honor the places where they met with God. These rocks and high places were meeting places, not dwelling places. Abraham's Mount Moriah was to become David's Mount Zion, God's dwelling place, but it was still only a mountain. Jacob may have called his stone pillow Beth-el—house of God, but it was still just a rock. Moses would be the one to build God a house, a moveable one, but still a dwelling place for the Most High, a *Tabernacle in the Wilderness*.

Model #1: Moses' Tabernacle

It is strange that the God who is everywhere present would desire a dwelling place on the earth. In the Scriptures, I see three dimensions of God's presence:

- » God's omnipresence—His presence in all of creation (Acts 17:28),
- » God's Inner Presence—His presence in the hearts of His people (2 Corinthians 6:16), and
- » God's Manifest Presence—His presence within the praises of His people (Psalm 22:3).

The house that Moses built was for this Manifest Presence—the revelation of the presence and sovereignty of God in a given place and at a given time. As the first Dwelling Place for God, this structure carries significance for all those who would make the journey into the Manifest Presence.

- » The worshiper entered the Tabernacle through a Beautiful Gate.
- » The Outer Court was the place of praise as psalms were chanted, proclaiming the glory of God. It was also the place of repentance and humility as sins were confessed and hearts were humbled before God.

> » In the first chamber of the Inner Court, the Holy Place, the priests kept a Table of Shewbread, representing the Presence and Word of God. There was also an Altar of Incense representing the prayers of the people of God and a Golden Lampstand to give light to the room. A heavy veil separated the two chambers of the Inner Court.
>
> » The inmost room was the Holy of Holies, also called the Most Holy Place, containing the Ark of the Covenant with the Mercy Seat, where, once a year, atonement was made for the sins of the nation. There was no window or lamp, but there was light, a divine immanence known as the shekinah, the glory of God. Strong defines the word kabowd, as "properly, weight, but only figuratively in a good sense, splendor or copiousness: -glorious (-ly), glory, honor (-able)."9 The word shekinah is not found in the Bible but in the rabbinic commentaries as the combination of sha*kan*, "to dwell," and *mishkan*, "the tabernacle."

This was the glory of God, the weight of the significance of His Dwelling Place given to the Israelites as the sign of their Covenant with God. This was the glory that departed from the Temple (Ezekiel 10:18-19), and this would be the glory promised to return with the Messiah (Haggai 1:8; Zechariah 2:10).

This was the glory announced by the angels to the shepherds the night Jesus was born and reported by eyewitnesses of Jesus like John, "We have seen his glory!" Through the grace of God in acceptance of the blood of innocent animals as atonement for the sins of the people, the Lord was able to manifest His presence, the weight of His Glory, the *kabowd*, there in that inmost room of Moses' Tabernacle.

So this Tabernacle, made of the reclaimed riches of Egypt, built by men as praise unto the Lord with skills learned in Egypt, and formed by the pattern sent from heaven, became the dwelling place of God on the earth.

The Pattern of Heaven Come to Earth

It gives us the pattern we follow into the Manifest presence of God. We enter through the Gates of Thanksgiving, and we proclaim His excellence in the Courts of Praise. We humble our hearts at the Brazen

---

9   Strong, James. "H3519 – kabowd." *The New Strong's Expanded Exhaustive Concordance of the Bible.* Red letter ed. Nashville, TN: Thomas Nelson, 2010.

Altar of Repentance. We enter the Holy Place to pray and to hear the Word in the light and power of the Holy Spirit (Altar of Incense, Table of Shewbread, Golden Lampstand). We pass through the Torn Veil into the Holy of Holies to wait in the presence of the King, to behold His glory and be changed.

We follow this same pattern because of who Jesus is.

> - He is the Beautiful Gate, and we enter in with thanksgiving.
> - Jesus is the perfect Lamb, slain once and for all so that our sins can be forgiven. Therefore, we can proclaim His excellence in the Outer Courts of Praise (Psalm 100).
> - He is the Shewbread in the Holy Place, the Living Word proclaimed to us and the divine presence available to us.
> - He lifts our prayers to the Father (Altar of Incense), and He has sent us the light and power of the Holy Spirit (the Golden Lampstand) to illumine our minds and empower our prayers.
> - Jesus is the Torn Veil (Hebrews 10:20), allowing us to enter the Holy of Holies. There, we find Jesus to be the Messenger of the Covenant and the Shekinah, the revelation of God to us.

The New Covenant Worship Paradigm, Worship/Word/Altar, fulfills this ancient pattern beautifully. Wherever you are reading this, the people you are called to reach can meet God through this pattern of worship. God's contemporary presence abides in this ancient Tabernacle of Worship.

Model #2: David's Tabernacle

The Lord has chosen to manifest His presence on the earth. One level of this manifestation is in nature, and another is the revelation of His nearness in our hearts. The most powerful, specific, and intimate is the Manifest Presence of the Lord, His presence within the praises of His people (Psalm 22:3). The Book of Psalms describes this level of worship. Every human emotion appropriate for worship is found in the Book of Psalms: joy and sorrow, pleasure and pain, confusion and faith, stillness and action, solitude and community. When led by the Holy Spirit, God's people can express these things in a necessary catharsis of soul and spirit and a requisite interaction of God's family with God Himself. This type of congregational worship is revealed to us by the model of David's Tabernacle. Moses' Tabernacle shows us the broad pattern of worship and our individual privileges and responsibilities as Priests unto the Lord. David's Tabernacle shows us the joy and significance of our ministry together as a Priesthood. Moses' Tabernacle is about worship and the worshiper; David's Tabernacle is about the worshiping community.

A Brief History

When King David brought up the Ark of the Covenant, his motive was to restore the presence of the Lord to the center of the nation and the hearts of the people. This was a direct outworking of the heart of David—he was called the man who was after God's heart. To me, this has two meanings:

1. David's heart was fashioned in the likeness of God's heart, and
2. David was a man who pursued the heart of God.

It is impossible to review the lives of David and Jesus and fail to see the similarities of each one's heart: a shepherd's heart, a humble heart, a heart shaped by the Word of God, a principled heart, and a heart hungry for the presence of God the Father in prayer and a heart broken by sin. We also see the passionate heart of David as he actively pursued the presence of God, just as Jesus did the presence of His Father.

A New Covenant

After a first, unsuccessful attempt when he failed to consult the Word of God on how the Ark should be moved, David succeeded in bringing up the Ark to Jerusalem (2 Samuel 6; 1 Chronicles 15,16). He did not place it back in the Tabernacle of Moses but placed it in a tent on Mount Zion instead. His view was that God had abandoned the old tabernacle (Psalm 78:67-72). Gone were the restrictions of the old tabernacle (men only, Jews only in the Outer Court; priests only in Inner Court). The Tabernacle of David was a foretaste of NT worship—"Whosoever will may come!" (Mark 8:34,35). This is why the prophets foretold the restoration of David's Tabernacle as a vital part of Messiah's ministry.

Isaiah predicted this:

> *In mercy the throne will be established; And One will sit on it in truth, in the tabernacle of David, Judging*

and seeking justice and hastening righteousness (Isaiah 16:5, NKJV).

Amos said this:

"On that day I will raise up the tabernacle of David, which has fallen down, and repair its damages; I will raise up its ruins, And rebuild it as in the days of old; That they may possess the remnant of Edom, And all the Gentiles who are called by My name," says LORD who does this thing (Amos 9:11–12, NKJV).

In Acts 15, at the first great church conference, the issue was the cultural make-up of the church. Was the church to be a Jewish sect, or was it to be an international group open to all races and levels of society? James settled the dispute by quoting the prophet Amos (Acts 15:12–22). Because the Messiah would bring back the glory as the fallen Tabernacle of David was restored, the church of Jesus Christ was to be universal, not just local. The Old Covenant was with the nation of Israel; the New Covenant was to be available to all mankind.

The New Testament and the Psalms

Paul and James tell us to sing Psalms. When we do the instructions found there, the Psalms become New Testament instructions. Tabernacle of David worship is New Covenant worship (in Spirit and Truth) as it is described in the Psalms: with reason and with emotion, corporate as well as individual, joyful as well as repentant, musical as well as literary, with movement as well as with stillness, loud as well as silent, questioning as well as affirming, in crisis as well as in the daily routine, with instrumental music as well as with vocal music, carefully planned and spontaneous, and with the arts of man as well as with the Word of God.

Corporate Worship and Mt. Zion

Just as personal worship was established at Moses' Tabernacle, corporate worship was established at David's Tabernacle. Our corporate worship (David's Tabernacle) must be underpinned by real and powerful personal worship (Moses' Tabernacle). Today, in every nation of the world, we need both. As the writer of Hebrews said, when the NT church worships, we

> ...have come to Mount Zion and to the city of the living God, the heavenly Jerusalem, to an innumerable company of angels, to the general assembly and church of the firstborn who are registered in heaven, to God the Judge of all, to the spirits of just men made perfect, to Jesus the Mediator of the new covenant, and to the blood of sprinkling that speaks better things than that of Abel (Hebrews 12:22–24, NKJV).

What an awesome privilege is ours to worship the Lord at the summit of Mount Zion, to join the songs of heaven with our earthly voices, to celebrate our King in His very throne room, and to spend time with Jesus, the mediator of the New Covenant. Joyfully, we ascend the hill of the Lord and stand in the Holy Place (Psalm 24).

As we open the ancient doors of praise, the King of Glory comes in!

For Class Discussion

1. How is the Tabernacle of Moses more than just an historical event?
2. How important is the worship progression in Moses' Tabernacle to today's worship?
3. Discuss the meanings of the rooms in Moses' Tabernacle to modern worship.
4. Discuss the additional truths added to OT worship illustrated in David's Tabernacle.
5. How did the prophecy of the restoration of David's Tabernacle settle the crisis in Acts 15?

CHAPTER 9
THE 7 BIBLICAL MODELS 3 & 4

Identity and Function

Model #3: The Holy-Royal Priesthood

The Lord warned Moses, high on the mountain, that things were not going well in the valley below.

Before he reached the foot of Mt. Sinai, the sound of "worship" reached his ears. He held in his hands the tablets of stone that would call for worship, with detailed instructions on how it should be done and what it would mean. Soon, the tablets would crash to the ground and break.

Who was leading the worship at the foot of the mountain? How was it being done? The answers to these questions would break Moses' heart and anger Almighty God. Up there on the mountain, Moses interceded for the people so recently ascended from Egyptian slavery. In the valley, Aaron, the brother of Moses, fashioned in gold a calf, and the people were "worshiping" with all their might. The wrath of God burned through Moses, and a worship purge left thousands dead and focused the nation on true worship—worship by the Book.

The orgy of "worship" also wrought a change, a delay, really, in the plan of God for mankind. Read the Lord's words at the giving of the Law and sense his plan for the world. "Although the whole earth is mine, you will be for me a kingdom of priests and a holy nation." (Exodus 19:5-6). Yet, after the worship of the golden calf, the Lord selected the sons of Aaron and the tribe of Levi to be a priestly tribe.

> *So, I will consecrate the tent of meeting and the altar and will consecrate Aaron and his sons to serve me as priests (Exodus 29:44).*

> *...appoint the Levites to be in charge of the tabernacle of the covenant law (Numbers 1:50).*

The terrible disobedience of people and the spineless "leadership" of Aaron postponed the plan of God all the way from the giving of the Law at Mt Sinai to the giving of his Son at Mt. Calvary. God's plan was for Israel to be a Kingdom of Priests, bringing salvation to the whole world. False worship temporarily put this plan aside, but what God intended at Mt. Sinai, He has accomplished at Mt. Calvary. The Apostle Peter makes it clear.

> ...you also, like living stones, are being built into a spiritual house to be a holy priesthood, offering spiritual sacrifices acceptable to God through Jesus Christ... But you are a chosen people, a royal priesthood, a holy nation, God's special possession, that you may declare the praises of him who called you out of darkness into his wonderful light (1 Peter 2:5, 9).

John's revelation shines a universal light on this Calvary-cleansed kingdom/priesthood.

> ...with your blood you purchased for God persons from every tribe and language and people and nation. You have made them to be a kingdom and priests to serve our God, and they will reign on the earth (Revelation 5:9–10).

Without a doubt, the church has been raised up out of the Egypt of sin to be this Holy Nation, the Kingdom of priests, the Holy, Royal Priesthood. We have a vital ministry to perform to the Lord Himself—True Worship. And we have a ministry to the world—telling them the Jesus Story. Under the old covenant, the priests had responsibilities in three broad areas:

1. worship and worship leading,
2. learning and teaching the Word of God, and
3. assisting in the processes of redemption.

These are also the areas of ministry for the new covenant priests.

Priests unto the Lord Worship God with Heart, Soul, Mind, and Strength

Individually, we are each a holy, royal priest unto the Lord. This truth frames and fuels our private worship, as we will develop later. When we gather to worship, we form the holy, royal priesthood. Without this theology of public worship, the focus of each event quickly moves to us: the songs we like, the ceremonies we prefer, the preaching that blesses us, the prayers that reinforce our comfort zones. We are quite willing to go to war over these preferences, deluding ourselves into thinking we are defending God's preferences. Actually, we are taking a seat-of-the-pants approach to worship, never questioning our self-centered motivations. It is ironic that people of the Book, with an announced philosophy of taking the Bible as the final authority in matters of faith and practice, would approach public worship from an if-it-feels-good-do-it point of view.

How transforming it would be if our worship leaders and rank-and-file worshipers would see themselves as priests unto the Lord, a Kingdom of Priests. Jesus would be the focus of every service. The Holy Spirit would have a free hand to move among us. The Lord Jesus would rule over us, granting miracles and deliverances, signs and wonders, saving the lost, restoring the weak, healing the sick, and calling people to lives of service. Ultimately, our public worship would impact the world, fulfilling the Jesus Agenda of Luke 4.

> *The Spirit of the LORD is upon Me, Because He has anointed Me to preach the gospel to the poor; He has sent Me to heal the brokenhearted, to proclaim liberty to the captives and recovery of sight to the blind, to set at liberty those who are oppressed; to proclaim the acceptable year of the LORD (Luke 4:18–19, NKJV).*

Is it too strong to say this? Our self-centered, me-oriented worship has this result: The poor are ignored; the broken-hearted continue in hopeless mourning; the captives remain safely out of sight in their prisons; the blind stumble on in their darkness; the oppressed never lose their bruising shackles, and the opportunities afforded by the Day of Grace are kept secret. The Holy Royal Priesthood worships God—do we?

Priests unto the Lord Know and Teach the Word of God

Make no mistake, priests, under both the old and new covenants, had the assignment of learning and teaching the Word of God. Self-centered worship is characterized by a dearth of Scripture and by a debilitating lack of Scriptural and theological thought behind the planning and execution of the services. Most of the time, leaders are just feeling their way from song to song, from service to service, and from season to season.

Called to a life of intimacy with God Himself and charged with the assignment of communicating and living out the Word of God, the Holy Royal Priesthood is a force for good in the world. We are holy through the Blood of Jesus, and we are royal because we serve in the courts of the King. Just as the old covenant priests assisted the people in the offering of their sacrifices to find reconciliation with God, new covenant priests give public witness to the claims of Christ as the final and ultimate sacrifice for all the sins of the world. As priests unto the Lord, we tell the Jesus Story to the world. We do this as we worship, as we preach, as we witness, and, most importantly, as we live. Great classical prayers of the church to be an excellent enhancement for my daily private worship.

As we open the ancient doors of praise, the King of Glory comes in!

Model #4: The Living Sacrifice of Praise

An Aroma Pleasing to the Lord

Every evening, every morning, throughout the centuries of Old Testament worship, the smoke of sacrifices coiled upward from the Tabernacle and later from the Temple. Every year the man of Israel, the priest of his home, would select from his flock the finest male lamb to offer to the Lord as a sacrifice on the Day of Atonement. Since it was the man's sins that required atonement, under the guidance of the priest, the man would slay the lamb himself. When the instructions for offering these sacrifices to the Lord are given in Leviticus, a strange statement is made repeatedly.

> *It is a burnt offering, a food offering, an aroma pleasing to the LORD (Leviticus 1:9).*

Does our God enjoy the smell of burning flesh and hair, of grain and oil?

Since God is spirit (John 4:24) the smells of the material world, so unavoidable to us, do not register in his awareness as they do in ours. What was the spiritual aroma that pleased him when an Old Testament worshiper put the knife to the lamb or lifted the grain and waved before the Lord? Jesus made it clear that true worship emanates from the heart; to worship the Father, who is Spirit, we must enter the realm of the Spirit and do so in truth. Under the New Covenant, our animals are safe from the knife and altar. The New Testament sacrifice is the sacrifice of praise. It is putting the knife to our own pride and self-reliance.

The fundamental biblical image of worship is that of the sacrifice.

In the Old Testament, the record is clear:

> - Unnamed animals died to provide the covering of Adam and Eve's sin-revealed nakedness.
> - Murder in the first family of earth entered the world through a heart that was not right, its error revealed by an improper sacrifice.
> - Animals in Noah's ark included in their number not just pairs for repopulating the earth but sets of sacrificial animals to mark the deliverance of mankind and the animal kingdom from the floods of God's wrath.
> - Abraham told his servants to wait while He and Isaac went some distance away to worship. He was talking about putting the knife to his only son at God's command.

The whole relationship of God with Israel was predicated upon constant sacrifices, day and night, and upon celebrating the great seasonal feasts throughout the year. King Saul lost his kingdom through an unlawful and rebellious "sacrifice." King David was chosen to be king in Saul's place because his heart was right. Later in life, David refused to offer a sacrifice on land given to him with these words, "I will not sacrifice to the LORD my God burnt offerings that cost me nothing" (2 Samuel 24:24).

Mary of Bethany

In the New Testament, Mary of Bethany offered Jesus a costly sacrifice of praise when she lavished her most prized possession on the Lord. She won His highest commendations.

- » "Why are you bothering this woman? She has done a beautiful thing to me" (Matthew 26:10).
- » "She did what she could" (Mark 14:8).
- » He also connected the preaching of the undiluted Word of God with this costly sacrifice of praise. "Truly I tell you, wherever the gospel is preached throughout the world, what she has done will also be told, in memory of her" (Mark 14:8–9).

> In Mark 14:8, Jesus also said, "She poured perfume on my body beforehand to prepare for my burial." The meaning of Jesus' death is that of the final sacrificial lamb.

Jesus' story is not the story of a young man tragically struck down by society; it is the story of a willing, perfect sacrifice. The writer of Hebrews explains that, like the material veil torn in the Temple at the moment of His death, Jesus' body was the spiritual veil torn to open the way for a fallen mankind to enter the presence of a Holy God. (Hebrews 10:19–25).

Paul exalted this costly sacrifice as the example for us in worship.

> *Have this attitude in yourselves which was also in Christ Jesus, who, as He already existed in the form of God, did not regard equality with God something to be grasped, but emptied Himself...He humbled Himself by becoming obedient to the point of death: death on a cross (Philippians 2:4–9, NASB).*

The aroma God loves is the spiritual scent of hearts being emptied before Him, the self-inflicted wounding of our human pride. As the Psalmist said,

> *My sacrifice, O God, is a broken spirit; a broken and contrite heart you, God, will not despise (Psalm 51:17).*

Romans 12:1–2 presents powerful promises to the one who would offer his humanity to the Lord as a living sacrifice. The destructive patterns of life in a fallen world will be broken. The worshiper's mind will be renewed, and he will prove the fullness of God's will. Somehow, this meager presentation of our fallen, wounded selves, this voluntary lifting up of our hearts, hands, and voices to Him in worship, is pleasing to God. Surely this is the "aroma pleasing to the Lord" Moses tells us about. No wonder Paul pleads with the Romans to enter into this sacrifice of praise. It is a reasonable thing to do.

The writer of Hebrews exalts the Sacrifice of Praise to the pinnacle of his exposition of the New Covenant.

> *Through Jesus, therefore, let us continually offer to God a sacrifice of praise—the fruit of lips that openly profess his name. And do not forget to do good and to share with others, for with such sacrifices God is pleased (Hebrews 13:15–16).*

This is more than the event described in Romans 12; this is a continual offering, a life-process like breathing. The attitude of praise (gratitude, humility) should be as consistent as respiration, a constant intake of heaven's atmosphere into our earthbound spirits. This will result in the fruit of our lips confessing His name and the fruit of our lives as we "do good and to share with others, for with such sacrifices God is pleased."

This is the Sacrifice of Praise, the "aroma pleasing to the Lord."

For Class Discussion

1. Describe how the OT Priesthood illustrates the ministry of the NT worshiper.

2. Discuss the statement NT priests are "holy by through the Blood of Jesus, and we are royal because we serve in the courts of the King."

3. Describe the ministry of the Holy Royal Priesthood: The Living Sacrifice of Praise.

4. Discuss the implications of Psalm 51:17 for the Living Sacrifice of Praise.

5. How important is it that the NT church is itself a priesthood?

CHAPTER 10
THE 7 BIBLICAL MODELS 5, 6, & 7

God's Response

But You are holy, enthroned in the praises of Israel. Our fathers trusted in You; They trusted, and You delivered them. They cried to You, and were delivered; They trusted in You, and were not ashamed (Psalm 22:3–5, NKJV).

Model #5: The Throne of God and of the Lamb

Extending the Kingdom of God

In Psalm 24, the Psalmist declares, "The earth is the Lord's, and all its fullness" (v. 1, NKJV). He asks the worship question of the ages, "Who may ascend into the hill of the LORD? Or who may stand in His holy place?" (Psalm 24:3, NKJV). He invites us to "Lift up your heads, O you gates! And be lifted up, you everlasting doors!" (Psalm 24:7, NKJV). He promises, "And the King of glory shall come in" (Psalm 24:9c, NKJV). Because the Lord is enthroned upon the praises of His people (Psalm 22:3) when we worship God (Psalm 24), the King does indeed "come in!" We sense His presence, that wonderful God-moment when anything might happen. The entrance of the King into our midst is the goal of every Pentecostal worship service. In very truth, we extend the Kingdom of God into our time and space by humbling ourselves before Him in praise and worship. The Lord responds to the humble heart turned toward Him with the wonderful gift of His presence, His sovereignty come to earth. In the words of the writer of Hebrews, "We have come to Mt. Zion!" The Bible gives us two detailed visions of the Throne of God and a three-point definition of what the Kingdom of God is in substance.

What Is It Like Before the Throne of God?

Looking to Isaiah chapter six and the Book of Revelation, we see what the Throne Room of God is like. It is a place where God is worshiped continually by angels, creatures, elders, and saints. The focus of the whole locale is the One Who Sits on the Throne. The will of God gets done here at the Throne of God. There is no rebellion, no self-centeredness, no straying minds or wandering eyes. Jesus is the center of all. There is unity of spirit and purpose, although men and women are there from every tribe and tongue and nation. Jesus has made them into one whole, worshiping family. There is continual music, confession, ceremony, and liturgy. And there is visual beauty beyond the mind of man to comprehend.

This brief description, inspired by the reports of Isaiah and John, reveals how off-centered and impoverished our worship has too often become. The desires and needs of man are at the center, not Jesus. Sometimes, our buildings are plain and unadorned, speaking inadequately of the intricate detail and monumental scope of the One we worship. Our motives, often a mixture of disunity and self-service, underlie our "offerings" of worship. We are surrounded by people who look and sound just like us, or we are divided into musical camps, each ignoring, if not despising, the other. Our services limp along with little content and less flow in a pale imitation of the grandeur and depth of the liturgy of heaven. With proud hearts on display and rebellious spirits in command, only lip service is paid to the will of God. How far we have drifted from the Throne of God!

The Sovereignty of God

But we have His promise. He will be enthroned upon our praise! If we humble our hearts and turn to Him and begin to invest our worship with the liturgy of heaven (the glory, worthiness, and majesty of King Jesus!), He will receive our worship to be His Throne!

We can know the joy and power of His sovereignty among us: His kingdom come, and His will done among us, here and now. Paul gives us the test of our worship in his definition of the Kingdom of God.

> *For the kingdom of God is not a matter of eating and drinking, but of righteousness, peace and joy in the Holy Spirit, because anyone who serves Christ in this way is pleasing to God and receives human approval (Romans 14:17–18).*

When we can look at the church and see these three characteristics at work (righteousness, peace, and joy in the Holy Spirit), then our worship is actually an extension of the Kingdom of God. But if there is hidden sin, or unrest and strife, or depression and discouragement, then some other king has come. His will is being done, not the Lord's.

Beholding His Glory

At the Throne of God, lives are changed. When we enter the realm of the splendor of His majesty and sovereignty, miracles, signs, and wonders happen. Worshipers, like the prophet Isaiah, hear the call of God to service. If we wonder why we have a dearth of miracles, signs, and wonders and why so few are hearing the call of God into a life of service, perhaps this is part of the answer. These things happen at the Throne of God. If our worship does not take us there, how can we know these blessings?

If we wonder why there is a dearth of character in the church, why the gifts seemed to be more important to some than the fruit of the Spirit, we must consider how far we are from the Throne of God. Paul said to behold the glory of the Lord was to be changed, just as Isaiah and John, our two witnesses, were never the same after their visions of the Throne of God.

> *But we all, with unveiled face, beholding as in a mirror the glory of the Lord, are being transformed into the same image from glory to glory, just as by the Spirit of the Lord. (2 Corinthians 3:18, NKJV).*

Lord, show us Your glory so that we might be changed!

Model # 6: The Office-Place of the Lord

A Place for Messiah to Do His Ministry

> *Now in the church that was at Antioch there were certain prophets and teachers: Barnabas, Simeon who was called Niger, Lucius of Cyrene, Manaen who had been brought up with Herod the tetrarch, and Saul. As they ministered to the Lord and fasted, the Holy Spirit said, "Now separate to Me Barnabas and Saul for the*

work to which I have called them." Then, having fasted and prayed, and laid hands on them, they sent them away (Acts 13:1–3, NKJV).

Ministry to the Lord

This biblical phrase, "minister to the Lord," is an absolute key to the understanding of worship. The NIV translates this as "worshiped the Lord," and that is a good translation. The Greek word is *"leitourgeo* (li-toorg-eh'-o); to be a public servant, i.e. (by analogy) to perform religious or charitable functions (worship, obey, relieve): KJV—minister.[10]" Vines contextualizes this definition in this way:

> leitourgeo NT:3008, (akin to A, No. 2), in classical Greek, signified at Athens "to supply public offices at one's own cost, to render public service to the State"; hence, generally, "to do service," said, e.g., of service to the gods. In the NT (see Note below), it is used (a) of the prophets and teachers in the church at Antioch, who "ministered to the Lord," Acts 13:2.[11]

At Antioch, this college of spiritual leaders engaged in fasting and worshiping the Lord, probably in a liturgical style, like the worship in the Temple, since this same word is used to describe that kind of worship in Hebrews 10:11. In fact, this Greek word is the source of the English word, "liturgy," etymologically meaning "the work of the people."

I find the literal meaning of the word *leitourgeo* to be a source of an exciting concept of worship. It is one of the seven biblical models of worship I develop in my book *Worship That Pleases God*, in seminars like *Enter In...*, and in the Fire and Form columns I write for my website, stevephifer.com. I call it the "Office-Place of the Lord."

The Office-Place of the Lord

The idea is simple enough: when we worship in Spirit and Truth, we provide the Lord with an earthly place to do His work. Our sanctuaries become His Office-Place when we truly worship Him. So do our lives, our

---

10 Strong, James. "G3011 – leitourgos." *The New Strong's Expanded Exhaustive Concordance of the Bible.* Red letter ed. Nashville, TN: Thomas Nelson, 2010.
11 Vine, W.E.. *Vine's Expository Dictionary of New Testament Words: A Comprehensive Dictionary of the Original Greek Words with their Precise Meanings for English Reader.* MacDonald Publishing Co., 1989.

workstations, and our homes; every capacity of life that is given over the Lord as praise and worship can be a place for Him to do His work in the world.

We are all familiar with the concept of the office.

- » When we move from assignment to assignment, we are not comfortable until our office is set up and running. I look around me now and see familiar books going back to high school and continuing through doctoral studies. I want this literary record of my studies here in my office.
- » Most of us will even have an office at home in addition to the one at work. In these are found the mementos of our journey, pictures and plaques of extreme significance, and tools of our ministry: the computer, the printer, the phone, the files.

Apply these familiar trappings of our work to the Lord Jesus and His work.

- » We are His office!
- » When we have made Him the Lord of our lives, or when we have ministered to Him, giving Him the place of preeminence in our services of worship, then He can work through us.

The Ministry of the Messiah

What is the Lord's work? It is the ministry of the Messiah as prophesied by Isaiah (Isaiah 61) and claimed by Jesus (Luke 4).

> *The Spirit of the LORD is upon Me, Because He has anointed Me to preach the gospel to the poor; He has sent Me to heal the brokenhearted, to proclaim liberty to the captives and recovery of sight to the blind, to set at liberty those who are oppressed; to proclaim the acceptable year of the LORD (Luke 4:18–19, NKJV).*

This is still His work today. When we minister to Him, He ministers through us.

- » He preaches the gospel to the poor using our organs of speech.
- » He uses our embrace to bind up the brokenhearted.
- » Our words proclaim the liberty of the captives in prisons of all sorts and new sight for eyes long blinded by sin.

> Those who are oppressed, bruised by the enemy of their souls with shackles that cruelly bind, are set at liberty by His power as we go about living for Him, following His call, seeking His anointing, telling His story, worshiping Him with heart, soul, mind and strength.

Worshipers are healers in this world.

Our words can be His words, our touch His touch, our embrace His loving caress. Worshiping churches are healing stations in this world, hospitals for the wounded heart. There is a work that only Jesus can do, but He has chosen to do it through His people. Is it any wonder the enemy of souls fights True Worship with every weapon He can muster? The Lord Jesus wants to set up His office in your life and mine, in your church and mine. Let us be faithful to minister to the Lord.

Model #7: The River of Life

The Flow of Healing Power in Worship

Scriptures Describing the River of Life:

> *Then he brought me back to the door of the temple; and there was water, flowing from under the threshold of the temple...And when the man went out to the east with the line in his hand, he measured one thousand cubits, and he brought me through the waters; the water came up to my ankles. Again he measured one thousand and brought me through the waters; the water came up to my knees. Again he measured one thousand and brought me through; the water came up to my waist. Again he measured one thousand, and it was a river that I could not cross; for the water was too deep, water in which one must swim, a river that could not be crossed. He said to me, "Son of man, have you seen this?" Then he brought me and returned me to the bank of the river...There will be a very great multitude of fish, because these waters go there; for they will be healed, and everything will live wherever the river goes (Ezekiel 47:1, 3–6, 9, NKJV).*

And he showed me a pure river of water of life, clear as crystal, proceeding from the throne of God and of the Lamb. In the middle of its street, and on either side of the river, was the tree of life, which bore twelve fruits, each tree yielding its fruit every month. The leaves of the tree were for the healing of the nations (Revelation 22:1–2, NKJV).

The River of Life is a Healing Stream. One of the most vivid images in Scripture of the power of worship is the River of Life, seen in Ezekiel 47 and Revelation 22, two strikingly parallel passages. Other references include the Psalms (1; 36, 46) and the words of Jesus (John 7:38).

Four Depths to Experience

In Ezekiel's vision, we see four depths to the river: ankle-deep, knee-deep, waist-deep, and water over the head. Ezekiel and his angel-guide passed through the first three levels but found the fourth depth to be too large to cross. It was a river in which one must swim. I observe four levels, or depths, in our common worship experience: thanksgiving, proclamation, adoration, and communion. These correspond to the four depths of the river in Ezekiel's vision. Here is my interpretation:

- » **THANKSGIVING:** We enter the ankle-deep waters of life when we give thanksgiving to the Lord. Psalm 100 identifies thanksgiving as the gateway to the presence of the Lord. Like standing ankle-deep in a stream, thanksgiving is refreshing to the soul. But this is a level intended as a passage, not for a dwelling place, so we go out deeper.

- » **PRAISE:** When we are standing knee-deep in a river, we can feel the current. In fact, we have to counter the force of the river with every step. When we go beyond thanksgiving and proclaim the Lord's excellence, His character, deeds, and love, we also move from refreshing to a state of being impressed with the Lord's power. Thanksgiving and praise refresh and impress us with God's power, but these are levels of expression that we must pass through.

- » **ADORATION:** When we move from knee-deep to waist-deep in the waters of life, to my mind, we are going from the proclamation of praise to the expression of adoration. We move from praise to worship, from speaking about God to speaking to Him, from an emphasis on what He has done for us to Who He is in us. Now, change begins. Learning from the image of wading into an ever-deepening river, it is clear that ankle-deep and knee-deep do not bring about lasting change. We can exit the river at the exact spot we entered. But the next passage to waters that are waist-deep begins the process of being altered by the waters. The river carries us downstream with every step. This explains why churches can be active in praise but still not progress toward the holiness the Lord expects from us. Praise is refreshing and impressive, but it is not transforming. Paul said that to contemplate His glory was to be changed (2 Corinthians 3:17–18). When we worship the Lord, we are changed. This, of course, takes time, time we are sometimes reluctant to allot to corporate worship. For decades, this time was found in those wonderful, long altar services in the American Pentecostal tradition. But, as the altar service has fallen out of vogue, we have put praise and worship on the clock, and we have lost the sense of tarrying, of waiting on the Lord. No wonder our strength is not often renewed.

» **COMMUNION WITH GOD:** Still, this incredible privilege of standing waist-deep in the waters of life is also a passageway and not a destination. Ezekiel's angel-guide brought him out another thousand steps. At this point, Ezekiel had to swim, let go of the safety of the riverbed, and launch himself into the presence of the Lord. The first result was that he got wet all over. Many of us know what this is in worship, to be immersed in the presence of the Lord. These experiences change us forever. This is the place where baptism in the Spirit happens, calls to the ministry are heard, miracles and healings take place, bondages are broken, and shackles of sin are destroyed. I am afraid the ranks of our churches are filled with people who have never been wet all over. This level of spirit-deep communion with God is still available to us in the secret place and in the public place. The river still flows in its fullness from the Throne of God and of the Lamb.

Do not abide in the shallows!

In Ezekiel's vision, the shallow marshes were not healed. His words are stark: "But its swamps and marshes will not be healed; they will be given over to salt" (Ezekiel 47:11, NKJV). I fear the shallow, me-centered, time-conscious worship of the contemporary church. Do you hear the Spirit calling us out farther into the waters of life? Do you hear Him calling us deeper?

That's where the healing is.

For Class Discussion

1. Discuss the importance of the concept that God responds to our praise and worship.

2. Psalm 22 says that God inhabits our praise and is enthroned upon our praise. Describe the differences between the two.

3. Discuss the concepts of ministry to the Lord and the resultant office-place of the Lord.

4. Explore the reality of the River of Life flowing from the Throne of God.

5. How does the author interpret the meaning of the four depths in the River of Life in relation to the worship of the church?

CHAPTER 11
SERVICE STRUCTURE

Three-fold Worship, a Form with Power

> *But mark this: There will be terrible times in the last days. People will be lovers of themselves...having a form of godliness but denying its power. Have nothing to do with such people (2 Timothy 3:1–2, 5).*

In my 10th-grade Biology class, I heard about an ecosystem—the simple pond of water in a field. The pond was the host to all manner of plant and animal life, from micro-organisms to fish to turtles to the small mammals who came to drink. Yet to take away any element of the environment, the oxygen in the water, the nutrients in the soil, or the sunlight shimmering on the water, was to destroy the whole thing. This is a picture of Pentecostal Worship—a spiritual ecosystem that supports supernatural life when all of its elements are in place.

Some would say my title is an oxymoron—a self-contradictory statement. Pentecostal *Structure?* "If one is led by the Spirit, one is certainly *not* structured." Really? "To be really *spiritual*, worship must be free of form." Again, *really*? As the title of this chapter indicates, we are seeking both fire *and* form, a structure that throbs with the power of God to change lives. The two quotes in this paragraph represent what is called an embedded theology within the ranks of classical Pentecostals. An embedded theology is a more cultural than spiritual phenomenon—a cherished belief we hold to without knowing when or where it was transmitted to us. It is a deeply held belief that has never been challenged by reason, measured against history, or tested by Scripture. Things we believe without Scriptural support and against all logic and experience are the theologies of church splits and wasted ministries. Arguments for embedded theologies are loud and emotional and lead to power plays and other less-than-the-Kingdom-of-God behaviors and tactics. Without Scriptural base or reasonable rationale, personalities and personal preferences take the stage, and what is thought to be a spiritual or theological debate is actually a culture clash.

Let's settle this now. God is a God of form. Psalm 19 reminds us that creation itself tells us about who the Creator is: a God of power and might and matchless form.[12] The forms of the universe are so precise that man can send a spaceship to the edges of the solar system and know exactly where everything will be at any given moment. In the 20th century, man even figured out that underlying this cosmic perfection, there is still a measure of random wisdom that only God can know. Amid universal precision, there is still room for the improvisational power of God. Physicists call this relativity; I call it sovereignty.

Creation is telling us of the nature of God, a Creator who flows through forms with His power. Paul's warning to Timothy was that in the last days, people would be self-centered, judging all of life by personal benefit. "What's in it for me?" will be the tenor of the times. When this outlook is applied to public worship, the result is what my mentor, Dr. Robert E. Webber, calls "narcissistic worship." This sickness can infect our songs, our services, and our souls. Each "worshiper" becomes the arbiter of what will and will not be done by what pleases him or, in more pseudo-spiritual terms, what "ministers" to him. Back in the 1970s, a popular song declared, "It can't be wrong if it feels so right." Now, to many in this new century, this unfortunate axiom has become the test of what is right and wrong in public worship. Narcissism robs worship forms of their godly power, leaving only the music and ceremony to limp along for an hour or so. Simply put, if the "worship" is about us, then it isn't about Him. We have lost the oxygen-rich soil and sparkling sun in our ecosystem, and our pond is drying up.

Three-Fold Worship

The 20th century brought something else to the world—the Pentecostal/Charismatic Renewal. I have wondered what the greatest contribution of Classical Pentecostalism to the church at large might be. Missions happened before the Pentecostal movement began. Sunday School and mass evangelism also predate it. The movement cannot claim the activity of the Gifts of the Spirit as its contribution since this is an Apostolic phenomenon. What then? It is a three-fold form of public worship: Worship/Word/Altar.[13] Judging from my own experience growing up in the Assemblies of God and from my study of Church

---

12 Psalm 19:1–2, NIV: "The heavens declare the glory of God; the skies proclaim the work of his hands. Day after day they pour forth speech; night after night they reveal knowledge. They have no speech, they use no words; no sound is heard from them."
13 This is purely my observation and not based on the work of any scholar.

history, we have discovered a form of public worship consisting of: a time of worship—the ministry of the congregation, followed by

1. the preaching of the Word—the ministry of the preacher, and
2. the Altar Service, a time of corporate and private prayer when everyone responds to the Word and Presence of God.

An Altar Service is more than an Altar Call.

The Altar Call, or Invitation, has a history that predates us. The Altar Service begins with an Altar Call but then takes on a life of its own. Years before the "Song Service" expanded into a time of "Praise and Worship," this is the part of the service where we learned to follow the moment-to-moment leadership of the Holy Spirit. Some unique elements of the Altar Service are:

» a lack of time-consciousness,

» a sense of waiting for God,

» a sense of dwelling in the presence,

» a spontaneity and flexibility, and,

» a blending of private and corporate prayer.

In these times of dwelling in the presence of God, with no thought of the clock, with personal involvement, and with a willingness to go wherever the Spirit would lead, the Pentecostal work of the Spirit gets done. People are healed, baptized with the Spirit, and are the beneficiaries of direct leadership of the Holy Spirit as they are called into the ministry. Relationships are repaired as forgiveness flows from wounded hearts to those who have done the injury. Addictions are broken and spiritual darkness lifts from the minds of God's people as chains of bondage fall before the power of God. The things on the Messiah's list in Luke 4/Isaiah 61 happen in our midst.[14]

Like the proverbial pond we all studied in high school biology, Pentecostal worship is a delicate, if powerful, environment. Each part of this spiritual ecosystem is essential to the fullness of the Life of the Spirit.

---

14 Isaiah 61:1-3, NIV: "The Spirit of the Sovereign LORD is on me, because the LORD has anointed me to proclaim good news to the poor. He has sent me to bind up the brokenhearted, to proclaim freedom for the captives and release from darkness for the prisoners, to proclaim the year of the LORD's favor and the day of vengeance of our God, to comfort all who mourn, and provide for those who grieve in Zion — to bestow on them a crown of beauty instead of ashes, the oil of joy instead of mourning, and a garment of praise instead of a spirit of despair. They will be called oaks of righteousness, a planting of the LORD for the display of his splendor."

> There must be worship—the ministry of the People of God (the liturgy). This must be treasured and protected from narcissistic corruption or outright neglect, like the oxygen in the pond's water.

> There must be anointed preaching of the Word—the ministry of the preacher. We possess an unction from the Spirit to present the Word of God with authority beyond our personalities and skills. This is like the nutrients in the soil around and under the pond.

> We must provide time for all of us to respond to the power of the Word of God in the preaching and the Presence of God in the Worship—the Altar Service. This is the ministry of the Holy Spirit to us and the ministry of the people to the Lord. This is like the shimmering sunlight dancing on the surface of the pond, giving life and beauty to all who draw near.

Worship/Word/Altar is a form of godliness full of the power of God for this new century.

For Class Discussion

1. Does the idea of Spirit-led worship imply a lack of form?
2. Should a worship service be planned ahead of time and rehearsed? Or should we just gather and see what happens?
3. Should the structure of a worship service reflect the nature of the God we are worshiping?
4. What has been your experience of the structure of worship services? Which ones worked and which ones did not?
5. Discuss the Classical Pentecostal Structure of Worship/Word/Altar.

CHAPTER 12

THE SWORD OF THE SPIRIT

Dividing Spirit from Soul

For the word of God is alive and active. Sharper than any double-edged sword, it penetrates even to dividing soul and spirit, joints and marrow; it judges the thoughts and attitudes of the heart. Nothing in all creation is hidden from God's sight. Everything is uncovered and laid bare before the eyes of him to whom we must give account (Hebrews 4:12–13).

"Don't run with that kitchen knife!" mother warned. "Be careful with that paring knife. Cut away from your body when you peel those potatoes," she further instructed us when we were little helpers in the kitchen. Sharp blades have to be handled with care to do the job for which they were intended. There is one particular blade that is so sharp it will divide soul from spirit, joint from marrow, and even our thoughts from our intentions. This blade is the Sword of the Spirit, the Word of God.

If we are to understand worship from a biblical point of view, we must let the Sword of the Spirit do its work. The images used by the writer of Hebrews show the internal work the Spirit of God wants to do in our lives: He wants to reveal the secret things, things that, if allowed to remain hidden, will hinder us, perhaps even ruin us. Let's take them one image at a time.

- » "Soul from spirit"—The Holy Spirit will show us through the Word of God which strong emotions within us originate in our spirit and which ones come from our souls.

- » "Joint from marrow"—In the human body, joints provide flexibility and utility, while marrow gives strength to the bones. Deep within us, we may not realize the differences between occasions to bend and occasions requiring unbreakable inner strength. The Word of God helps us know when to flex and when to stand firm.

> "Thoughts from intentions"—Modern therapists say we have a conscious mind (thoughts) and a subconscious mind (motives). The Holy Spirit uses the Sword of the Spirit to reveal hidden motivations that drive us to say one thing and do something else.

We have been cleansed by Calvary's blood and made new creatures in Christ Jesus. The Lord does not plan for us to spend the rest of our days as slaves to unseen motives, untrue beliefs, and uncontrollable inner drives. Jesus wants to set us free from these hidden chains.

What does this have to do with worship? Everything. Many worshipers "feel" about worship, but rarely do they "think" about worship. Some never question their own strong feelings. Strong feelings can spring from the cleansed spirit within us as we are compelled and inspired by the Word of God, but they can also spring from wounded souls, fearful hearts, and errant theologies.[15]

Emotions are commanded by Scripture. Music, the principal art of worship, is the language of emotions. What the Bible has to say about worship forms our theology, but the minute we express what we believe, we do so in cultural terms. Culture can be the language of the soul or the spirit. Our feelings and our culture must be judged by the Word of God.

Our souls, like our bodies, have fallen into sin. When we receive Jesus into our lives as Savior, the Holy Spirit quickens our spirit as we experience a new birth. As we grow in the Lord, that same Spirit works to sanctify us from the inside out to cleanse us from ungodliness and set us apart to God.

That means hidden fears can be quelled in Jesus, unseen shackles can fall behind us, and compulsive behaviors can be overcome. Unrecognized controlling forces often compel us to do things beyond our control. These horrid things grow in the dark places in our wounded souls when evil words are not forgotten, deep bruises still bleed, unspoken appetites continue to clamor and secret sins still molder. But things that grow in the dark die in the light.

The Word of God, like a blade of blinding light, is the only sword sharp enough to divide soul from spirit, joint from marrow, and thought from intention. The same Jesus Who cleanses our sinful record from the heavenly books wants to forgive our secret sins, heal our deepest bruises, and free our souls from anything that would bind us.

15 In my thinking, "soul" refers to the self and sense-conscious parts of us: emotions, memories, passions, and preferences. "Spirit" refers to the God-conscious part of us where Jesus lives by the power of the Holy Spirit as He reveals spiritual truths to us.

Chapter 12—The Sword of the Spirit

If we are to cleanse our worship culture from the effects of ungodly influences, we must look within our own hearts. Three questions help us do that:

1. Will I worship to please myself? Have I allowed my preferences to take the prominent place in my worship choices? Paul warned that those controlled by sinful nature cannot please God (Romans 8:5-11).

2. Will I worship to please others? Do I make my choices in worship based on what I think other people expect of me? Again, Paul says, "Am I now trying to win the approval of human beings, or of God? Or am I trying to please people? If I were still trying to please people, I would not be a servant of Christ" (Galatians 1:10).[16]

3. Will I worship to please God? Is my passion focused on the Lord, His work, His will, and His way?[17]

When we can answer question number three with a heartfelt "Yes!", we are on our way to the discovery of the essence of life itself, the life lived in the resurrected power of Jesus Christ, the "Spirit and Truth" worship life. Jesus wants to complete the work of Calvary and cleanse our hearts. He wants to touch our sulking, wounded souls and rob our wounds of their controlling power over us. He wants to show us how strong we can be when our spiritual bones are full of rich marrow as His powerful blood flows in us. At the same time, He wants to show us we are strong enough to be flexible when we need to bend to His will. Also, He wants to hear us sing and make the music of heart He loves so much as soul and spirit unite in redeemed culture as we lift our voices to Him.

We must not fear this sharp blade or shrink back from the loving hand of the One who wields it. This is a blade we can run with safely!

---

16 Also see: 1 Thessalonians 2:4–6
17 See 1 Thessalonians 4:1–8; 1 Timothy 2:4–6; and Hebrews 11:5–6

For Class Discussion

1. What is your understanding of the trinity of the human being: body, soul, and spirit?
2. Discuss the differences between the soul (the self-conscious part of us) and the spirit (The God-conscious part of us.)
3. Why do these two inner realities need to be separated by the Word of God?
4. Discuss the differences between folks who "feel" about worship and those who "think" about worship.
5. Discuss the three questions:
   - Will I worship to please myself?
   - Will I worship to please others?
   - Will I worship to please God?

CONCLUSION
THE CONGREGATIONAL CHALLENGE

Beyond the Comfort Zone

Public Worship Should Stretch the Worshiper

The Comfort Zone

Each of us has one. Physically, there is a space that surrounds us we feel is ours. When some uninvited person invades this space, we feel crowded and uncomfortable. If possible, we will retreat and reestablish the zone, our comfort zone. This zone also exists in other aspects of life. In relationships, in finances, in neighborhoods, and even in our homes, we establish comfort zones. Our loved ones know where the boundaries are: the subjects not to bring up, the chair not to sit in, the spending limit, the habits not to challenge. We approach these zones only with caution and at great personal risk.

Comfort in Public Worship

These comfort zones can be found in the church as well. The house of God can become such a comfortable place. We know all the people, all the songs, and all the routines. Relationships are secure, roles are well-defined, and the calendar is a model of consistency. Serving Jesus is such a pleasant life.

Really? Has the Lord Jesus claimed us as His own, filled us with His Spirit, and called us to His Kingdom just to establish and reinforce better comfort zones? Yes and no.

Yes

In one sense, yes. There is a spiritual security zone maintained by the Lord.

- We are hemmed in by His love. "You have hedged me behind and before, and laid Your hand upon me" (Psalm 139:5, NKJV).
- This zone is intended to make us secure in our relationship with God.
- We can live consistent Christian lives knowing that the circumstances that confront us have to cross God's desk first.
- We can face each day with confidence, and we can actually take joy in trials knowing that God is at work through the circumstances we face.

If the story of Job illustrates life for us, even the spiritual forces who oppose us have lines they cannot cross.

Each of us lives within a Divinely ordained security zone.

No.

But this is not the whole story. Within the protection of a divine security zone, God can allow us to be quite uncomfortable.

- Under this canopy of grace, the Holy Spirit often challenges us to stretch beyond the personal comfort zones we have established.
- In Isaiah 54:2, the Lord speaks to Israel as if she were a barren woman, "Enlarge the place of your tent, and let them stretch out the curtains of your dwellings; do not spare; lengthen your cords, and strengthen your stakes" (NKJV).
- Many of us have established our own comfort zones well within the boundaries of those God has set.

It Is Time to do Something

2 Kings 7:3 tells of four starving lepers outside the city gate in a time of war and famine. When they realized that there was no hope for them in the city, they fled to the Syrian city. What they didn't know was that God had routed the enemy. The four lepers helped themselves to a feast. Their decision to break out of their pitifully painful comfort zone was expressed this way: "Why stay here until we die?" (NIV).

Let us be as smart as those poor lepers. Why should we sit around in our comfort zones while the feasting table of God is available to us?

How the Holy Spirit longs to shake us from our lethargy, to interrupt our routines, to invade our services, and to enlarge our hearts. Why? Because, like ancient Israel, barrenness accompanies the contented community. Comfort zones isolate us from potential blessings and potential brothers and sisters.

Learning to Stretch

How can we "stretch out the curtains of our dwelling?" Truth stretches us. How many years have we been studying the Bible, yet there is always a new truth, or an old truth from a new angle, or an as yet undiscovered stream of Biblical witness that stretches a familiar truth into new areas of application.

As truth is rehearsed in our hearts and minds, one of the intended effects is growth in our concepts of God and His Kingdom: "stretching out the curtains" as we "enlarge the place of our tent."

How is truth rehearsed in our hearts? Several important ways:

- » Bible reading, Bible study, Bible teaching, and Bible preaching spring to mind.
- » But there is another way that must take its rightful place on this list: Bible singing.

When the New Testament tells us to sing psalms, we are being instructed to sing Scripture. Singing is a powerful teaching tool because the music adds an emotional element that opens the heart to the truth. Certain elements of music, such as meter, melody, and repetition, make memorization easier. These are natural allies to the process of ingesting the truth of the song. In corporate settings, the unity of all the believers singing the same truth at the same time with the same emotion is a vital force in the life of the church.

Two Ways to Sing the Word

There are two types of Bible singing:

1. scriptures set to song and
2. songs composed to express Biblical truths.

To the composer, the challenges of each type of song are exciting. Setting verses of Scripture to music is a great challenge. Composing songs to express Biblical truths is a different type of challenge.

Singing Scripture, when approached systematically, will stretch us beyond our comfort zones. In a musical sense, singing Scripture is a challenge to the worshiper, but it is worth the effort.

- » When we learn to sing Scripture, we are hiding God's Word in our hearts. We can be assured that when we need that truth, it will be in our hearts and on our lips as we sing God's answer to our dilemma.
- » Complex songs with lots of words and verses challenge a congregation as well. Some choose not to use them, preferring the songs that yield an immediate return within that service.
- » As a worship leader, I consider it worth the service time to sing an involved song of important truth often enough until it has its effect.

This is worth the effort. Great theology can be infused into the hearts of God's people through the great art of composers of today and the past.

At Ease in Zion

The Bible warns us against getting too comfortable in worship. The prophet Amos said,

Woe to you who are at ease in Zion (Amos 6:1, NKJV).

One of the great signs of ease is singing on automatic pilot, where the singer doesn't need to see the words because he has sung this song since childhood.

A Challenging Technique

Paul reported a balance in his worship life.

...I will pray with the spirit, and I will also pray with the understanding. I will sing with the spirit, and I will also sing with the understanding (1 Corinthians 14:15, NKJV).

There were times when his song was a song for his spirit to sing and other times when it taxed him mentally. We need both kinds of song as well. Worship of Almighty God should release our spirits to soar in worship and challenge our minds to new concepts of God.

Conclusion—The Congrgational Challenge

Worship should stretch us beyond our comfort zones.

For Class Discussion

1. Discuss the role of comfort in worship.
2. In what ways does True Worship stretch the worshiper?
3. What do you think about singing Scripture songs?
4. What does it mean to be "at ease in Zion?"
5. Are you able to echo Paul's determination to be faithful in public worship (1 Corinthians 15:15)?

To Continue Your Biblical Study of Worship

The Wonder of Worship is the product of years of study and experience in the role of the Pastoral Artist. I pray these additional resources will be useful to you in your ministry to the Lord.

A Website Packed with Worship Study Materials:

Over 400 essays and articles designed to shed the Light of Scripture on these issues of artistry, integrity, ministry renewal, prayer, private devotions, and ministry resources.

A Website with Private Devotions for each Day of the Week:

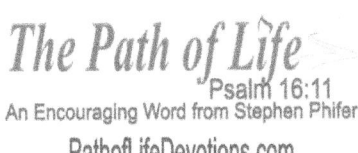

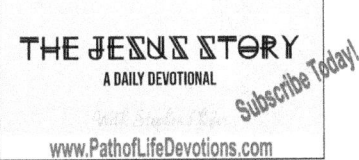

Consider these books by Stephen Phifer:

Available directly from the author DrStevePhifer@Gmail.com
or from the publisher at kingdomwindspublishing.com/shop/

Public Worship   Private Worship   Personal Prayer

The Nativity   Worship Team   Worship Arts

Worship Arts Resources from Stephen Phifer

May the Lord be pleased with your Ministry to Him!

-Steve

www.ingramcontent.com/pod-product-compliance
Lightning Source LLC
Chambersburg PA
CBHW072219070526
44585CB00015B/1402